"Many people who have shifted to a healthy plant-based diet have told me that the hardest food for them to do without is quality ice cream. Now, thanks to Jeff Rogers, you can make your own gourmet frozen desserts without dairy products. And they'll taste better than Ben & Jerry's or Baskin-Robbins ever did!"
—JOHN ROBBINS, author of *Diet for a New America* and *The Food Revolution*

"Quite delicious. . . . We enjoyed the taste test and felt honored to be among the first to try this exciting cruelty-free dessert. We are all nut lovers, so the Maple Walnut was a huge hit. "
—INGRID E. NEWKIRK, president of People for the Ethical Treatment of Animals (PETA)

"Sinfully sumptuous, fun to make, and all vegan! That's one improvement in ice cream that's long overdue."
—DR. NEAL BARNARD, president of the Physicians Committee for Responsible Medicine and author of *Power Foods for the Brain*

"An impressive addition to the world of delicious, healthy desserts that adds pleasure to life without artery-clogging cholesterol and saturated fat. Jeff's recipes are simply and sinfully great."
—FRANCIS JANES, international restaurateur

"Jeff Rogers doesn't just give you a slice, but a whole spoonful of heaven with his amazing frozen dessert recipes. His creations are delicious and unforgettable. Yum!"
—SABRINA NELSON, WebWitch, VegSource.com

"*Vegan Ice Cream* shrinks the fallacy that a chasm exists between nutritional food and good tasting food. Jeff does an amazing job of proving through his work that we can both enjoy our food and live healthy at the same time!"
—JERROD SESSLER, cancer survivor and author of *Food Chains* and *Five Percent Chance*

"Jeff Rogers creates decadent ice creams that match, even surpass, their dairy counterparts. His ice cream recipes are perfect for people who can't digest dairy or just want to live a healthier lifestyle."
—TAL RONNEN, chef/owner of Crossroads, Los Angeles, and author of *New York Times* best-seller *The Conscious Cook*

VEGAN ICE CREAM

VEGAN
ICE CREAM

Over 90 Sinfully Delicious
Dairy-Free Delights

JEFF ROGERS

PHOTOGRAPHY BY CLARE BARBOZA

Previously published as *Vice Cream*

TEN SPEED PRESS
Berkeley

Contents

Acknowledgments

Thanks to Zel and Reuben Allen for all of their help and guidance. As someone who rarely uses recipe books, I appreciate the time and effort you offered to help bring my recipe book to fruition.

Thank you to my mother, Dottie; my brothers, Paul and Sam; and all of my friends and relatives for their support on this project.

A very special thank you goes to Bill Amey, my good friend and cofounder of SoyStache.com, for all of his support, his friendship, and especially his sense of humor. He will be missed.

Thanks to the wonderful staff at Ten Speed Press.

And thank you to all who dedicate their lives to helping others improve theirs, whether through diet or otherwise, as well as to those who strive to inform and educate so that others may make truly informed decisions.

Introduction

In my younger years, I consumed a lot of ice cream and favored the rich flavors of Ben & Jerry's, whose factory happened to be in the neighboring town. Over the years, I experimented with my diet and discovered the effect of foods on my overall health. While moving toward a plant-based diet, I reduced (and later eliminated) my migraine headaches, and my high blood pressure returned to normal. I also had far fewer colds and fewer instances of the flu. Their severity and duration were also much less. After I discovered the benefits of a vegan diet, I found that the vegan "ice creams" on the market were simply not satisfying; they were not rich enough for me, and I did not enjoy the aftertaste.

Since there are many people who cannot eat dairy and many more who choose not to for ethical, environmental, and health reasons, I wanted to create a wonderful ice cream alternative. For those who were already vegans, this would add a new dessert to their diets. For others, it would allow them to give up the dairy they had been wanting to do without.

I thought that there must be a way of making a rich, flavorful vegan ice cream that would easily satisfy the expectations I had developed when I ate dairy. Having used cashew milk to replace cow's milk and cream in other recipes, I realized that was how I should make my homemade vegan ice cream. In 1999, I moved to Seattle, purchased an ice cream maker, and began experimenting with vegan ice creams. The results were as rich as I wanted them to be. A luscious, homemade vegan ice cream was finally born!

I began sharing these ice creams at local EarthSave potlucks and at other EarthSave chapters in cities like Vancouver, Canada; Portland, Oregon; and San Diego, California, as well as at WorldFest in Los Angeles. I soon had many people asking for my recipes or for the ice cream itself. Over time, I've traveled to many vegan, raw, and health food shows to demonstrate how delicious vegan ice cream can be and how easy it is to make. Sharing this healthful alternative to dairy ice cream has become part of my life's work. In the years since I first started making vegan ice creams, veganism has become much more popular. Vegan products have become more available in stores and online, plus vegan options at restaurants have greatly increased.

I soon realized that I'd rather distribute my recipes widely than produce vegan ice cream commercially, because using organic cashews, the base for many of the recipes, is rather expensive, and allowing people to make vegan ice cream themselves would make it more affordable. I believe that these recipes will make a difference in people's lives.

I certainly hope they succeed in doing so.

BASICS

SWEETENERS

I created these recipes to suit my own taste in sweetness, but feel free to adjust them according to your preference. Consider adding sweetener to a recipe gradually, to taste. You are also welcome to mix and match sweeteners to suit your preferences. For additional sweetness, the water in any recipe can be replaced with fresh juice, such as young coconut water or grape juice. As fruits vary in flavor and sweetness, you may need to adjust a recipe's sweetener accordingly.

I have long loved maple syrup and used it as the primary sweetener in my recipes, although as I've moved toward more raw and fresh ingredients in my cooking, I frequently use fresh dates as my primary sweetener. I prefer Grade A Amber Color and Rich Taste (formerly called "dark fancy") maple syrup; it offers a wonderful sweetness without overpowering the ice creams. The darker colored maple syrups have a stronger flavor and are known for offering more nutrients.

Other sweeteners can be substituted for maple syrup, though those such as Sucanat or dates will change the consistency of the mixture and may require that you thin it with additional liquid. You may substitute 1 cup of maple syrup with 1 cup coconut syrup, ¾ cup agave nectar, 1½ cups Sucanat, 1½ cups coconut sugar, or 1 cup packed organic pitted dates.

For raw vegan ice creams, I prefer to use dates in place of maple syrup. When using dates, I usually select Medjool, honey, halawi, or sometimes black dates, though other varieties can also be substituted. I've found honey and halawi dates to be very versatile, working well in most recipes. Darker dates, like Medjool and black dates, have a stronger flavor that works well in some recipes, but they tend to overwhelm vegan ice creams that have subtler flavors. The skins of the dates may produce some speckling in your ice cream; if you wish to avoid this, just remove the skins before blending. Soft dates may be used without soaking, but they might make the ice cream mixture too thick, in which case just add some liquid.

Dry pitted dates do not work well on their own and generally need soaking. Measure out the dates, then loosen them and transfer them to a jar. Add enough purified water to cover them. Place the jar in the refrigerator, to prevent fermentation, for several hours or overnight. Strain, reserving the sweet soaking liquid. To add extra sweetness, you may want to use the soaking liquid in place of some of the other liquids in a recipe, or you can save it for another use.

Brown rice syrup doesn't have the same sweetening ability as these other ingredients, but it can work well when mixed with another sweetener, such as maple syrup. For those who wish to use brown rice syrup, I suggest mixing brown rice syrup and maple syrup in equal parts, then adjusting to taste.

Diabetics and those who prefer not to use sweeteners that contain sugars can try using stevia, an all-natural dried herb, which is available in refined powder and liquid forms. Several types of stevia, however, have a licorice flavor that overwhelms some recipes. Some stevia powders are still green, and others have been refined. The green type is likely to be more natural, but it has the stronger flavor. Try using about 1½ teaspoons stevia in place of 1 cup maple syrup (see the Carob Stevia recipe on page 43). Stevia alone may not be sweet enough, so if you want to try stevia and don't object to the use of other sweeteners, you can use a combination of stevia along with maple syrup or dates. This combination offers sweetness with reduced sugars.

EXTRACTS

Use only alcohol-free extracts in ice cream recipes, as those with alcohol will inhibit the mixture's ability to freeze. The flavorings I use are available in most health food stores and are actually labeled "flavors," not "extracts." Frontier Natural Products has a nice line of natural flavors.

APRICOT KERNELS

In many of my recipes, I use almond flavor. In addition to being a fine flavor on its own, almond is a wonderful companion to chocolate, especially when married with vanilla. For raw versions of ice cream, you can use apricot kernels, sparingly, for a wonderful amaretto flavor. Apricot kernels are actually used commercially for creating the flavor in amaretto liqueur. I save the pits from the apricots I eat over the summer. I scrub them clean, dehydrate them, and store them in an airtight jar for future use. When I need one, I use a pair of pliers to crack it open. There is usually one teardrop-shaped kernel inside each pit. Please be careful: the shells are hard and can shatter.

CHOCOLATE CHIPS

I prefer smaller chocolate chips than those commonly available, and I've tried a variety of methods—food processors, coffee grinders, and even manual graters—for creating the ideal chips for my recipes. The trick is to break the chocolate into smaller pieces without the heat from the process melting the chips. What seems to work best is to chill the bowl and slicing blade of a food processor in the freezer and then use them to process room-temperature chips. When I've chilled the chips, they've been too hard to properly slice. Even with this method, I end up with chips of various sizes. If you don't have a food processor, use a knife and cutting board to chop the chips. Or, if you find a good bulk vegan chocolate or even a vegan chocolate bar, you can grate it with a hand grater.

Before adding chocolate chips to your vegan ice cream recipe, always chill them in your freezer for at least 15 minutes.

COCONUT MILK

Juicing the meat of mature coconuts is the best way to achieve an amazingly decadent coconut milk, though of course you could also use canned coconut milk. Unlike coconut water, which comes directly from the coconut, coconut milk requires some preparation. You may substitute coconut milk, in part or in full, for the cashews and water in my recipes.

To make 4 cups coconut milk, you'll need about 7 cups shredded fresh coconut (2 large coconuts) and 3 cups coconut water. The easiest way to shred the coconut meat is in a food processor. Stop the machine and scrape down the sides of the bowl occasionally as you process the coconut for about 3 minutes.

Once you have shredded the coconut meat, combine it with the coconut water in a blender and blend until very smooth. If your blender heats up with sustained blending, this is okay, as warming the mixture slightly (up to 100°F) helps the fiber release the fats into the mixture. You may need to turn it off and on periodically and tap your blender to remove air pockets near the blade. Add more coconut water if your blender has difficulty blending the mixture. Keeping the mixture thick will result in a richer coconut milk.

To juice the pulp manually, place the mixture in a nut milk bag and squeeze the milk out. To juice the pulp mechanically, run it through a juicer two or three times, to make sure you extract all of the milk.

If mature coconuts are not available or are too difficult to use because of the hard shells and meat, you still don't have to use canned coconut milk. Young coconuts are not as rich and flavorful as mature coconuts, but they are easier to use, offer some of the flavor, and can be substituted for coconut milk. Replace the coconut milk in the recipe with a blended mix of young coconut meat and young coconut water. The ratio should be about one part coconut meat to three parts coconut water.

After making your ice cream, you can drink any extra coconut milk straight or add it to a smoothie or sauce. If you compost, you should know that coconut shells, mature or young, don't break down very quickly. If you have a fireplace or enjoy campfires, try throwing the shells into the fire (it's fun to watch them burn because they flare up and produce subtle color changes). It is best to dry out young coconut shells prior to burning, as they have moist husks, so leave them out in the sun for a few days.

For a pictorial description of making coconut milk, please visit TheNaughtyVegan.com.

An alternative way to make raw coconut milk is to use raw dried shredded coconut. This will not taste exactly the same as fresh but is a great alternative. Blend about 4 cups raw shredded coconut and 5½ cups purified water until very smooth and slightly warm. Follow the above instructions for extracting the milk.

COCONUT, TOASTED

To prepare toasted coconut, place a sauté pan over medium heat. Pour 1 to 2 teaspoons coconut oil into the pan. When the oil is hot, toss in 1 cup shredded, unsweetened coconut. Stirring constantly with a wooden spoon, heat until the coconut is light golden brown, being careful not to burn it. If the coconut starts browning too fast, remove the pan from the heat and keep stirring. When browned, transfer it to a plate to cool. Store the toasted coconut in an airtight container in the freezer so that it's chilled and ready to use in an ice cream recipe.

COCONUT WATER

Coconut water is the liquid drained from the inside of fresh coconuts, with no alterations. It can be found in both young and mature coconuts, with slightly different flavors. The water from young coconuts usually tastes much sweeter and fresher. Be sure to read the recipes carefully; some call for coconut milk (see page 9), others for coconut water. Pasteurized coconut water is now widely available but will have a different flavor than fresh. There is also now available at some health food stores raw unpasteurized coconut water, though it is fairly pricey. If available, fresh coconut water is preferred over pasteurized. To learn how to open both young and mature coconuts, see my instructions with pictures at TheNaughtyVegan.com.

DURIAN

Three of these ice cream recipes (Coconut Durian, page 86; Coconut Cacao Durian, page 87; and Coconut Strawberry Durian, page 88) call for durian, a fruit from Southeast Asia that can be found in many Asian grocery stores and other markets that carry exotic fruits. It's shipped to the United States frozen, so you may find it in the freezer section. Durian is a large, thorny, hard-skinned fruit containing four or five sections of fleshy fruit, each enclosing several large seeds. A 7-pound durian will yield about $2\frac{1}{2}$ pounds edible fruit, though each fruit may vary. When the fruit is ripe and at room temperature, you can pull apart some of the thorns to create a tear in the skin, exposing the fruit within. Be careful, as the thorns are sharp and can cut skin. You can also cut the durian open with a knife, which is a little safer. Be warned that durian is also called "stinky fruit." It has a very distinctive odor, sometimes mistaken for natural gas. As an alternative to the whole fruit, durian is often available in the freezer section of Asian markets. It can be found in 1-pound plastic shrink-wrapped packages. These don't have the convenient compostable "wrapper" of the whole fruit, and cost more per pound, but I have found these to be consistently sweet and much easier to work with. Any leftover durian can be stored in the refrigerator in an airtight container.

GINGER JUICE

To make fresh ginger juice, pass peeled fresh ginger through a juicer, press it in a garlic press, or grate and squeeze it. In a pinch, you can also use plain grated ginger, grated using the smallest holes possible. I usually make up a large batch of juice in my juicer and then freeze it for future use. Six ounces fresh ginger will yield about 3 ounces juice, or about 6 tablespoons.

NUT MILKS

Raw vegan ice creams call for nut milks, such as almond and hazelnut milk. I use a juicer to produce the nut milk. If you wish to achieve a smoother texture, you can pour the milk through a fine-mesh bag after juicing. This method takes some extra effort, but it works well. Using a nut milk bag also gives you the option of adding a whole vanilla bean when blending the milk. That way, you get the full flavor of the bean while removing any remaining fiber from the pod. Because cashews are softer and less fibrous than almonds or hazelnuts, cashew milk does not require this extra step, though you are welcome to pass it through a nut milk bag to be absolutely sure of removing any remaining nut pieces that may affect the texture.

Please note whether a recipe calls for soaked nuts. In general, ³/₄ cup nuts, such as almonds, will expand to about 1 cup after soaking.

To make 4 cups almond milk, soak 5½ cups raw organic almonds overnight in enough water to cover, plus another third. The next day, drain and rinse the nuts. Using a sturdy blender or food processor, blend the nuts with 5 cups purified water until smooth. If necessary to keep your blender moving, add some extra water. Depending on your blender, you may also need to blend it in smaller batches. Pass the mixture through a juicer or a nut milk bag. (Depending on the juicer, you may need to feed the pulp through a second time to extract all of the milk.) Measure out the amount needed for the recipe, reserving the remainder for another use.

To make 4 cups hazelnut milk, replace the almonds with 5 cups raw organic hazelnuts.

To make 4 cups pecan milk, replace the almonds with 4 cups raw pecans and blend the nuts with only 4 cups purified water.

To make 3½ cups pistachio milk, replace the almonds with 2 cups raw pistachios and blend the nuts with 3 cups coconut water.

To make about 5 cups hemp milk, there is no need to soak the hemp seeds. Simply blend 3 cups raw hemp seeds with 4 cups purified water. I do not have a specific recipe for using hemp milk but want to provide this option for those with nut allergies or sensitivities. Feel free to try this milk in any of the vegan ice cream recipes. Hemp milk has a nutty flavor, but it's a stronger taste than the other dairy-free milks in this book.

While different "milks" may offer a different flavor to a recipe, feel free to mix and match the base nut milk, especially if you or those you're serving are not able to consume a specific nut, such as cashews.

If you don't use your nut milks right away, store them in an airtight container in the refrigerator and shake them well before using. They should last 2 or 3 days but are best used when fresh. To extend the shelf life, I put the fresh nut milk in the freezer for about an hour to quickly chill it and then transfer it to the refrigerator.

SPIRULINA POWDER

The color of mint and pistachio ice cream in its natural form is more white than green. Many mint and pistachio ice creams found in the supermarket achieve their vivid green hue through the use of artificial food colorings. If you want your ice cream to be green but wish to avoid artificial ingredients, a natural alternative is spirulina powder. Available at health food stores, spirulina is a green microalgae that is high in protein and commonly thought of as a "superfood." Adding ¼ teaspoon to your recipe will produce a subtle green color; adding ½ teaspoon produces a deeper green. In these small quantities, it minimally affects the flavor of the ice cream, if at all.

VANILLA

I call for vanilla in many of my recipes. While my preference is to use only the seeds from fresh vanilla beans, you may use whole vanilla beans or natural vanilla flavor instead. Vanilla flavor is a liquid flavoring, similar to vanilla extract but without the alcohol (alcohol can negatively affect the ice cream recipes). Vanilla flavor is convenient to use, while the vanilla seeds and whole beans offer fresher, stronger flavor. Using the whole bean is easier than scraping out the seeds and may provide additional flavor (most of the flavor comes from the seeds, but there is some extra oil and flavor in the pod), but it also adds tiny fibers to the recipe. Whichever form of vanilla you use is a matter of personal preference.

To use the seeds, I slice the beans lengthwise with a sharp paring knife and scrape the seeds from each half using the back of the knife blade. I then add the seeds into the mixture. I either discard the pods or, if my dehydrator is on, I'll place the pods inside to infuse my kitchen with vanilla aroma. To use the whole bean, one option is to cut the bean into pieces, then grind it into a powder in a clean coffee grinder before adding it to the ice cream mixture. Depending on the ability of your blender, a cut-up or whole bean may be added directly to the blender along with the other ice cream ingredients without needing to grind it first. Another option is to blend a cut-up bean with some liquid in a 1-cup blender jar before adding it to the larger blender. As a final alternative, there are now companies selling vanilla bean powder, so the grinding has already been done for you.

When using vanilla seeds or whole beans, you'll need a quarter to one whole vanilla bean for many recipes, depending on your taste. Vanilla beans can vary from region to region, and vanilla flavors can vary from company to company. Use your own taste to establish the right flavor balance for you. To substitute one form of vanilla for another in a recipe, here are approximate equivalences: 1 bean = 1 teaspoon vanilla powder = 1 to 2 teaspoons vanilla flavor.

RAW FOODS

I've devoted an entire chapter to raw vegan ice creams for raw foodists and those focusing on fresher and less processed ingredients. Since most cashews are heated during the shelling process, some raw foodists will not eat them. Truly raw cashews (shelled mechanically) are available in some health food stores, as well as online or via mail order, though they are more expensive. If you can eat raw cashews, then you will be able to adapt some of the nonraw recipes as well. Or you can try using some almond milk (page 13), fresh coconut milk (page 9), hazelnut milk (page 14), or a combination as a substitute.

To adapt the nonraw vegan ice cream recipes, you'll also need to substitute another sweetener for the maple syrup. I recommend soft pitted dates or soaked dry pitted dates (see page 7) in the raw recipes, but you may also use raisins or grape juice for sweetening. Agave nectar is also now available in a raw form.

JUICING

I use a Champion juicer made by Plastaket Manufacturing Company. I also use the Green Star juicer made by Green Power. There are many others on the market with varying functions and efficiency. The Champion is a masticating juicer, which chews the food to break down the fibers and squeeze out the juice. The Green Star is a twin auger juicer, which crushes and presses the food to break down the fibers and squeeze out the juice. Other juicers are centrifugal, with either angled mesh baskets that throw your pulp into a container, or mesh baskets with vertical sides that require periodic cleaning if you're working with a large batch of produce.

If you do not have a juicer, a food mill can be used to puree fruit and remove the skin and seeds, but be aware that the volume and texture of the juice may differ. For example, grape juice from a food mill won't taste the same as grape juice from a juicer, because removing the seeds changes the flavor. Also, because juicers have finer screens, using a food mill may make the juice thicker and may extract less liquid.

Some fruits, such as grapes and apples, can simply be shredded or grated, placed in a nut milk (fine-mesh) bag, and squeezed. For soft fruits, such as strawberries, it may be best to simply use the same amount of packed fruit as the juice called for in the recipe. Although it adds an extra step to your preparation time, you may wish to peel fruits such as peaches before use, as the skins can thicken your mixture too much without adding extra flavor or texture. If your ice cream mixture does turn out too thick, add some liquid, such as purified water.

BLENDING TIPS

Before freezing, the consistency of your ice cream mixture should be somewhere between a cream and a thin pudding. It's important that the mixture be very smooth, so add a minute or two to the suggested blending time if your mixture is still gritty. Another way to ensure a smooth texture is to first blend the nuts with a minimal amount of liquid to get them very smooth, then gradually add the remaining liquid called for in the recipe.

You can also soak the nuts overnight in purified water to soften them, which will help them blend more smoothly. If you soak the nuts, cut back slightly on the water or other liquid used in the recipe to maintain the proper consistency. Soaking the nuts may alter the flavor slightly. It may also make them easier to digest for those who have a difficult time digesting nuts.

Many of these ice cream mixtures, especially those used to make raw ice creams, are quite thick. If your blender seems to have trouble with the nuts or you are not getting good results, then try chopping the nuts in a food processor or by hand before adding them to the blender. You can also run the nuts through a masticating juicer with a blank screen to make a nut butter before blending. Also helpful is starting and stopping the blender to loosen up the ingredients around the blade. Another option is to divide the mixture in half and blend it in two batches.

If you use a very powerful blender, like Vitamix, you can add tough ingredients such as dates all at once in the beginning, rather than needing to add them one at a time.

Most of the sauce recipes in the last chapter of the book call for a 1-cup blender jar, which is placed upside down to fit over your traditional blender. It isn't required, but it does a better job of mixing thick ingredients in small quantities because it's smaller than a standard blender jar. Some pint jars actually fit blender blade assemblies and can be used for quantities up to 2 cups. As an alternative, you can also try an immersion blender.

ICE CREAM MAKERS

There are a variety of ice cream makers available on the market. There are two main types of makers: traditional salt-and-ice ice cream makers and newer makers that contain built-in coolant. Traditional ice cream makers typically have a 4- or 6-quart capacity, so for large batches, they are the way to go. Manual makers need to be cranked, so they require a lot of physical exertion, while electric models are much easier to use.

Ice cream makers with built-in coolant need to be placed in the freezer to chill overnight before using. I simply store mine in there so it'll always be ready for the next batch of ice cream. You then take out the ice cream maker, put in the blade and the motor, turn it on, and add your mixture to the canister. This is a very simple way to make a quart of ice cream, since it doesn't require the extra salt and ice, nor does it require a lot of attention or work. These makers are also available with manual cranks.

There is a third type of ice cream maker to consider, though it is usually more expensive. It is self-contained, so no salt or ice is needed. You also do not need to prefreeze anything. Just plug it in and it will mix and freeze your ice cream. For more information on choosing an ice cream maker, visit TheNaughtyVegan.com

SERVING INSTRUCTIONS

It's always best to serve your ice cream right after making it, if possible. If the ice cream has been stored in the freezer, you'll need to let it rest at room temperature for 10 minutes or more before serving it. Alternatively, you can place the frozen ice cream in the refrigerator for 30 minutes to 1 hour to gently soften. Vegan ice cream tends to freeze fairly hard and tastes best when softened a bit.

STORAGE

The fresher the ice cream, the better it is, of course, although I've kept pints in the freezer that were still tasty after several months. When packing your ice cream into storage containers, try not to leave too much air, which creates frost. Consider using multiple small containers, so that you can empty one container in a sitting and leave full containers for later. If you are not likely to use a full quart quickly, then using multiple smaller airtight containers will extend the freshness of your ice cream.

A list of online sources for ingredients and equipment for making vegan ice cream can be found at TheNaughtyVegan.com.

ICE CREAM

Vanilla Delight 24

Chocolate 25
CAROB
CHOCOLATE MINT
CAROB MINT

Chocolate Chip 26
CAROB CHIP
MINT CHOCOLATE CHIP
MINT CAROB CHIP

Chocoholic Delight 28
CAROB DELIGHT

Brownie Chocolate Chip 31

Chocolate Pecan 32
CAROB PECAN

Espresso 34
ESPRESSO MINT

Mocha 35
MOCHA MINT

Coconut Macaroon 36
CHOCOLATE COCONUT
  MACAROON
COCONUT MACAROON
  CHOCOLATE CHIP

Peanut Butter 39
PEANUT BUTTER
  CHOCOLATE CHIP

Almond 40

Maple Walnut 41

Date Nut 42

Carob Stevia 43
CHOCOLATE STEVIA

Strawberry 45

Strawberry Rhubarb 46

Raspberry 47

Blueberry 48

Peach Nectar 51
APRICOT NECTAR

Banana 52

Fresh Lemon 53
LEMON

Apple Cinnamon 54

Gingersnap 55

Peppermint 57

Jalapeño Heaven 58

Black Forest 59

Pumpkin 60

Carrot Cake 62

Vanilla is the classic ice cream flavor we all know and love. This version has all the creaminess and smooth, rich flavor of the familiar staple without any of the dairy. Enjoy it on its own, topped with some fresh chopped fruit, or coated with one of my sauces (see pages 118–28). (See page 29 for photo.)

Vanilla Delight

2 vanilla beans, sliced and scraped (see page 15)
2 cups organic cashews or cashew pieces
2 cups purified water
1 cup maple syrup

MAKES ABOUT 1 QUART

Combine the scraped vanilla bean seeds, cashews, water, and syrup in a blender. Blend on high until silky smooth, at least 1 minute.

Place the blender in the freezer for 40 minutes to 1 hour or in the refrigerator for at least 1 hour or up to overnight, until well chilled. Pour the mixture into an ice cream maker and freeze according to the manufacturer's instructions. Serve immediately or transfer to airtight containers and store in the freezer until ready to serve.

VEGAN ICE CREAM

If vanilla is the most popular ice cream flavor, then chocolate is its bolder, sultrier counterpart. This version of chocolate ice cream is smooth, rich, and luxurious. Chocolate lovers won't miss the dairy.

Chocolate

1³/₄ cups organic cashews or cashew pieces
1³/₄ cups purified water
1 cup maple syrup
2 teaspoons alcohol-free vanilla flavor
¹/₄ teaspoon alcohol-free almond flavor
¹/₂ cup unsweetened cocoa powder

MAKES ABOUT 1 QUART

Combine the cashews, water, syrup, vanilla flavor, and almond flavor in a blender. Blend on high until silky smooth, at least 1 minute. With the motor running, add the cocoa powder and blend until evenly distributed.

Place the blender in the freezer for 40 minutes to 1 hour or in the refrigerator for at least 1 hour or up to overnight, until well chilled. Pour the mixture into an ice cream maker and freeze according to the manufacturer's instructions. Serve immediately or transfer to airtight containers and store in the freezer until ready to serve.

CAROB Replace the cocoa powder with ¹/₂ cup unsweetened carob powder.

CHOCOLATE MINT Add 2 teaspoons alcohol-free peppermint flavor to the blender with the other liquid ingredients.

CAROB MINT Replace the cocoa powder with ¹/₂ cup unsweetened carob powder and add 2 teaspoons alcohol-free peppermint flavor to the blender with the other liquid ingredients.

When I was growing up, a couple of my favorite ice cream flavors were chocolate chip and mint chocolate chip. I loved the snappy crunch of chocolate chips against the smooth vanilla or cool mint base. When I became vegan, these common favorites were not available to me. Finally, I perfected a vegan version of these chocolate chip varieties that both satisfied my long-standing cravings for my old favorites and brought back childhood memories.

Chocolate Chip

1 cup organic vegan chocolate chips (see page 9), chopped
1¹/₂ cups organic cashews or cashew pieces
1¹/₂ cups purified water
1 cup maple syrup
1¹/₂ teaspoons alcohol-free vanilla flavor
¹/₈ teaspoon alcohol-free almond flavor

MAKES ABOUT 1 QUART

Place the chocolate chips in the freezer to chill.

Combine the cashews, water, syrup, vanilla flavor, and almond flavor in a blender. Blend on high until silky smooth, at least 1 minute.

Place the blender in the freezer for 40 minutes to 1 hour or in the refrigerator for at least 1 hour or up to overnight, until well chilled. Pour the mixture into an ice cream maker and freeze according to the manufacturer's instructions. Remove the cover and blade from the ice cream maker and fold in the chocolate chips, distributing evenly. Serve immediately or transfer to airtight containers and store in the freezer until ready to serve.

CAROB CHIP Replace the chocolate chips with 1 cup carob chips, chopped.

MINT CHOCOLATE CHIP Add 2 teaspoons alcohol-free peppermint flavor to the blender with the other liquid ingredients. Add ¼ to ½ teaspoon spirulina powder for color (optional, see page 15).

MINT CAROB CHIP Replace the chocolate chips with 1 cup carob chips, chopped, and add 2 teaspoons alcohol-free peppermint flavor to the blender with the other liquid ingredients. Add ¼ to ½ teaspoon spirulina powder for color (optional, see page 15).

For the passionate chocolate lover, a simple chocolate ice cream may not be enough. Here I kick it up a notch by including chocolate chips, which add a delightful crunch to the creamy chocolate base and pander to the true chocolate addicts among us.

Chocoholic Delight

1 cup organic vegan chocolate chips (see page 9), chopped
1¹/₂ cups organic cashews or cashew pieces
1¹/₂ cups purified water
1 cup maple syrup
1 tablespoon alcohol-free vanilla flavor
¹/₂ teaspoon alcohol-free almond flavor
¹/₂ cup unsweetened cocoa powder

MAKES ABOUT 1 QUART

Place the chocolate chips in the freezer to chill.

Combine the cashews, water, syrup, vanilla flavor, and almond flavor in a blender. Blend on high until silky smooth, at least 1 minute. With the motor running, add the cocoa powder and blend until evenly distributed.

Place the blender in the freezer for 40 minutes to 1 hour or in the refrigerator for at least 1 hour or up to overnight, until well chilled. Pour the mixture into an ice cream maker and freeze according to the manufacturer's instructions. Remove the cover and blade from the ice cream maker and fold in the chocolate chips, distributing evenly. Serve immediately or transfer to airtight containers and store in the freezer until ready to serve.

CAROB DELIGHT Replace the chocolate chips with 1 cup carob chips, chopped, and replace the cocoa powder with ¹/₂ cup unsweetened carob powder.

When I moved to Seattle, I discovered that the local co-op had a wonderful vegan brownie with chocolate chips. I would occasionally pick one up along with some vanilla soy milk for a hearty and indulgent snack. I realized the textures of the brownie and chips would both contrast and complement the dreaminess of chocolate ice cream. Combine these two for a sinful pleasure.

Brownie Chocolate Chip

1 cup crumbled vegan chocolate chip brownie
1 1/2 cups organic cashews or cashew pieces
1 1/2 cups purified water
1 cup maple syrup
1 tablespoon alcohol-free vanilla flavor
1/2 teaspoon alcohol-free almond flavor
1/2 cup unsweetened cocoa powder

MAKES ABOUT 1 QUART

Place the crumbled vegan chocolate chip brownie in the freezer to chill.

Combine the cashews, water, syrup, vanilla flavor, and almond flavor in a blender. Blend on high until silky smooth, at least 1 minute. With the motor running, add the cocoa powder and blend until evenly distributed.

Place the blender in the freezer for 40 minutes to 1 hour or in the refrigerator for at least 1 hour or up to overnight, until well chilled. Pour the mixture into an ice cream maker and freeze according to the manufacturer's instructions. Remove the cover and blade from the ice cream maker and fold in the crumbled brownie, distributing evenly. Serve immediately or transfer to airtight containers and store in the freezer until ready to serve.

The buttery-rich pecan is made tempting when paired with sultry chocolate. Serve this ice cream with Coconut Sauce (page 121), which has caramel undertones, to capture the flavors of decadent chocolate turtle candies.

Chocolate Pecan

1 cup chopped organic pecans
1^1/$_2$ cups organic cashews or cashew pieces
1^1/$_2$ cups purified water
1 cup maple syrup
2 teaspoons alcohol-free vanilla flavor
^{1}/$_4$ teaspoon alcohol-free almond flavor
^{1}/$_2$ cup unsweetened cocoa powder

MAKES ABOUT 1 QUART

Place the pecans in the freezer to chill.

Combine the cashews, water, syrup, vanilla flavor, and almond flavor in a blender. Blend on high until silky smooth, at least 1 minute. With the motor running, add the cocoa powder and blend until evenly distributed.

Place the blender in the freezer for 40 minutes to 1 hour or in the refrigerator for at least 1 hour or up to overnight, until well chilled. Pour the mixture into an ice cream maker and freeze according to the manufacturer's instructions. Remove the cover and blade from the ice cream maker and fold in the pecans, distributing evenly. Serve immediately or transfer to airtight containers and store in the freezer until ready to serve.

CAROB PECAN Replace the cocoa powder with ^{1}/$_2$ cup unsweetened carob powder.

For those of us who enjoy our morning coffee, the world is a better place when we can bring that flavor to a rich and creamy ice cream. Garnish with a vegan cookie—a molasses cookie will stand up well to the strong, distinctive notes of coffee.

Espresso

1 vanilla bean (optional), sliced and scraped (see page 15)
¼ teaspoon alcohol-free almond flavor (optional)
2 cups organic cashews or cashew pieces
2 cups purified water
1 cup maple syrup
2 tablespoons freshly ground organic espresso beans

MAKES ABOUT 1 QUART

Combine the scraped vanilla bean seeds, almond flavor, cashews, water, syrup, and ground espresso beans in a blender. Blend on high until silky smooth, at least 1 minute.

Place the blender in the freezer for 40 minutes to 1 hour or in the refrigerator for at least 1 hour or up to overnight, until well chilled. Pour the mixture into an ice cream maker and freeze according to the manufacturer's instructions. Serve immediately or transfer to airtight containers and store in the freezer until ready to serve.

ESPRESSO MINT Add 2 teaspoons alcohol-free peppermint flavor to the blender with the other liquid ingredients.

There is something soothing and magical about the combination of coffee and chocolate. The sweetness and bitterness of the flavors balance to make a warming, sophisticated treat evocative of the indulgent café beverage. For a fun presentation, serve this ice cream in a tall glass, dollop with vegan whipped topping and a sprinkling of cocoa powder, and garnish with a vegan biscotti.

Mocha

2 cups organic cashews or cashew pieces
2 cups purified water
1 cup maple syrup
$1/4$ teaspoon alcohol-free almond flavor
4 teaspoons freshly ground organic espresso beans
$1/4$ cup unsweetened cocoa powder

MAKES ABOUT 1 QUART

Combine the cashews, water, syrup, almond flavor, and ground espresso beans in a blender. Blend on high until silky smooth, at least 1 minute. With the motor running, add the cocoa powder and blend until evenly distributed.

Place the blender in the freezer for 40 minutes to 1 hour or in the refrigerator for at least 1 hour or up to overnight, until well chilled. Pour the mixture into an ice cream maker and freeze according to the manufacturer's instructions. Serve immediately or transfer to airtight containers and store in the freezer until ready to serve.

MOCHA MINT Add 2 teaspoons alcohol-free peppermint flavor to the blender with the other liquid ingredients.

I love coconut! My love affair with the exotic flavor began as a youth when my mother would bake macaroons for me and my brothers. This ice cream is delicious on its own, but it is divine with some fresh Chocolate Sauce (page 120) drizzled over it. Garnish with shredded coconut.

Coconut Macaroon

1 cup toasted shredded unsweetened coconut (see page 11)
1 cup organic cashews or cashew pieces
1^3/$_4$ cups coconut milk (see page 9)
1 cup purified water or young coconut water (see page 11)
1 cup maple syrup
2 teaspoons alcohol-free vanilla flavor
^{1}/$_8$ teaspoon alcohol-free almond flavor

MAKES ABOUT 1 QUART

Place the toasted coconut in the freezer to chill.

Combine the cashews, coconut milk, water, syrup, vanilla flavor, and almond flavor in a blender. Blend on high until silky smooth, at least 1 minute.

Place the blender in the freezer for 40 minutes to 1 hour or in the refrigerator for at least 1 hour or up to overnight, until well chilled. Pour the mixture into an ice cream maker and freeze according to the manufacturer's instructions. Remove the cover and blade from the ice cream maker and fold in the toasted coconut, distributing evenly. Serve immediately or transfer to airtight containers and store in the freezer until ready to serve.

continued

CHOCOLATE COCONUT MACAROON After the ingredients have been blended smooth, add ½ cup unsweetened cocoa powder and blend until evenly distributed.

COCONUT MACAROON CHOCOLATE CHIP (Pictured on previous page.) After the mixture has frozen, fold in 1 cup chilled organic vegan chocolate chips (see page 9), chopped.

When I was growing up, smooth peanut butter spread in
a thick layer between two pieces of whole-wheat bread and
then grilled was my preferred lunch on cold winter weekends.
This ice cream captures the creamy texture and earthy,
comforting flavor of peanut butter. It's instant nostalgia in a bowl.

Peanut Butter

1 cup organic cashews or cashew pieces
2 cups purified water
1 cup maple syrup
2 teaspoons alcohol-free vanilla flavor
$1/8$ teaspoon alcohol-free almond flavor
1 cup smooth natural peanut butter

MAKES ABOUT 1 QUART

Combine the cashews, water, syrup, vanilla flavor, and almond
flavor in a blender. Blend on high until silky smooth, at least
1 minute. With the motor running, add the peanut butter and
blend until evenly distributed.

Place the blender in the freezer for 40 minutes to 1 hour
or in the refrigerator for at least 1 hour or up to overnight,
until well chilled. Pour the mixture into an ice cream maker
and freeze according to the manufacturer's instructions. Serve
immediately or transfer to airtight containers and store in the
freezer until ready to serve.

PEANUT BUTTER CHOCOLATE CHIP After the mixture has
frozen, fold in 1 cup chilled organic vegan chocolate chips
(see page 9), chopped.

I've always loved almonds, in a variety of forms, whether in amaretto cookies, almond croquettes, or eaten on their own. This is a subtle and soothing flavor, great for a warm summer day or any time of the year. Match the ice cream with a vegan almond or pecan cookie, or contrast it with a chocolate cookie.

Almond

2 cups organic cashews or cashew pieces
2 cups purified water
1 cup maple syrup
1 teaspoon alcohol-free almond flavor

MAKES ABOUT 1 QUART

Combine the cashews, water, syrup, and almond flavor in a blender. Blend on high until silky smooth, at least 1 minute.

Place the blender in the freezer for 40 minutes to 1 hour or in the refrigerator for at least 1 hour or up to overnight, until well chilled. Pour the mixture into an ice cream maker and freeze according to the manufacturer's instructions. Serve immediately or transfer to airtight containers and store in the freezer until ready to serve.

Maple syrup is the signature agricultural product of Vermont, where I grew up, and woodsy, robust maple was one of my favorite flavors when I was a kid. Here, crisp bits of walnut add some sweet bite to the buttery maple base. This ice cream captures the classic flavor of my youth, although I do not recall it tasting quite this good!

Maple Walnut

1¼ cups chopped organic walnuts
1½ cups organic cashews or cashew pieces
1½ cups purified water
1 cup maple syrup
¼ teaspoon alcohol-free maple flavor

MAKES ABOUT 1 QUART

Place the walnuts in the freezer to chill.

Combine the cashews, water, syrup, and maple flavor in a blender. Blend on high until silky smooth, at least 1 minute.

Place the blender in the freezer for 40 minutes to 1 hour or in the refrigerator for at least 1 hour or up to overnight, until well chilled. Pour the mixture into an ice cream maker and freeze according to the manufacturer's instructions. Remove the cover and blade from the ice cream maker and fold in the walnuts, distributing evenly. Serve immediately or transfer to airtight containers and store in the freezer until ready to serve.

When I was growing up, my mother would often make date bars. With their tender, sticky date filling and buttery crumb topping, these old-fashioned bars were a beloved after-school treat. This recipe captures the sweetness of dates and counterbalances it with the buttery autumnal crispness of pecans. Garnish the ice cream with your favorite chopped nuts.

Date Nut

1 cup chopped organic pecans
1¼ cups organic cashews or cashew pieces
2 cups purified water
¼ cup maple syrup
2 teaspoons alcohol-free vanilla flavor
¼ teaspoon alcohol-free almond flavor
1 cup packed organic pitted Medjool dates (see page 7)

MAKES ABOUT 1 QUART

Place the pecans in the freezer to chill.

Combine the cashews, water, syrup, vanilla flavor, and almond flavor in a blender. Blend until smooth. With the motor running, gradually add the dates and blend on high until silky smooth, at least 1 minute.

Place the blender in the freezer for 40 minutes to 1 hour or in the refrigerator for at least 1 hour or up to overnight, until well chilled. Pour the mixture into an ice cream maker and freeze according to the manufacturer's instructions. Remove the cover and blade from the ice cream maker and fold in the pecans, distributing evenly. Serve immediately or transfer to airtight containers and store in the freezer until ready to serve.

This recipe offers a flavorful ice cream with a lower sugar content. Fruit has a natural sweetness without the spike of refined sugars, and stevia brings its own sweetness to the ice cream without the sugar or calories of traditional sweeteners. Try different fruits to take advantage of what's in season.

Carob Stevia

2 cups organic cashews or cashew pieces
2¼ cups purified water
1½ teaspoons stevia (see page 7)
1½ teaspoons alcohol-free vanilla flavor
¼ teaspoon alcohol-free almond flavor
1 cup mashed slightly overripe organic banana or other fruit,
such as packed hulled organic strawberries (optional)
½ cup unsweetened carob powder

MAKES ABOUT 1 QUART

Combine the cashews, water, stevia, vanilla flavor, and almond flavor in a blender. Blend on high until silky smooth, at least 1 minute. Add the banana and blend until smooth. With the motor running, add the carob powder and blend until evenly distributed.

Place the blender in the freezer for 40 minutes to 1 hour or in the refrigerator for at least 1 hour or up to overnight, until well chilled. Pour the mixture into an ice cream maker and freeze according to the manufacturer's instructions. Serve immediately or transfer to airtight containers and store in the freezer until ready to serve.

CHOCOLATE STEVIA Replace the carob powder with ½ cup unsweetened cocoa powder.

One of the brightest of the summertime fruits, strawberry makes for a delicious and satisfying dessert! For some added texture and color, chop several strawberries and freeze for at least 15 minutes, then mix them into the finished ice cream. Garnish with strawberry slices.

Strawberry

24 ounces (about 6 cups) fresh organic strawberries, hulled
1¹/₂ cups organic cashews or cashew pieces
1 cup maple syrup

MAKES ABOUT 1 QUART

Run the strawberries through a juicer to make 2½ cups juice.

Combine the strawberry juice, cashews, and syrup in a blender. Blend on high until silky smooth, at least 1 minute.

Place the blender in the freezer for 40 minutes to 1 hour or in the refrigerator for at least 1 hour or up to overnight, until well chilled. Pour the mixture into an ice cream maker and freeze according to the manufacturer's instructions. Serve immediately or transfer to airtight containers and store in the freezer until ready to serve.

A traditional combination most commonly found in pie, juicy strawberries and puckery rhubarb marry well in a creamy, fruity-tart ice cream. The cashews offer a wonderful smoothing of the flavors. This ice cream is refreshing on a hot day; garnish with strawberry slices.

Strawberry Rhubarb

12 ounces (about 3 cups) fresh organic strawberries, hulled
14 ounces fresh organic rhubarb (about 5 stalks)
1^1/$_2$ cups organic cashews or cashew pieces
1 cup maple syrup

MAKES ABOUT 1 QUART

Run the strawberries through a juicer to make 1¼ cups juice. Run the rhubarb through a juicer to make 1¼ cups juice.

Combine the strawberry juice, rhubarb juice, cashews, and syrup in a blender. Blend on high until silky smooth, at least 1 minute.

Place the blender in the freezer for 40 minutes to 1 hour or in the refrigerator for at least 1 hour or up to overnight, until well chilled. Pour the mixture into an ice cream maker and freeze according to the manufacturer's instructions. Serve immediately or transfer to airtight containers and store in the freezer until ready to serve.

During the summers of my youth in Vermont, my family used to collect raspberries from our backyard, and my mother would make fresh raspberry jam. During the process she would dish up some vanilla ice cream and top it with warm fresh raspberry jam for impromptu sundaes. This recipe captures the bright pairing of raspberry and vanilla and the summery festivity of those childhood desserts.

Raspberry

1 1/2 cups organic cashews or cashew pieces
1 1/2 cups purified water or fresh raspberry juice
1 cup maple syrup
2 teaspoons alcohol-free vanilla flavor
1/4 teaspoon alcohol-free almond flavor
1 cup organic raspberries

MAKES ABOUT 1 QUART

Combine the cashews, water, syrup, vanilla flavor, and almond flavor in a blender. Blend on high until silky smooth, at least 1 minute. With the motor running, gradually add the raspberries and blend until smooth.

Place the blender in the freezer for 40 minutes to 1 hour or in the refrigerator for at least 1 hour or up to overnight, until well chilled. Pour the mixture into an ice cream maker and freeze according to the manufacturer's instructions. Serve immediately or transfer to airtight containers and store in the freezer until ready to serve.

A powerhouse among the berry family, blueberries are not just nutritious but also colorful and refreshing! For a fun summertime treat, layer some of this fresh blueberry ice cream with chilled Blueberry Sauce (page 128) in ice pop molds and then freeze (as pictured, opposite). This recipe requires that you juice the blueberries; if you don't want to go to the trouble of juicing, replace the 2 cups blueberry juice with 1 cup chopped blueberries, increase the cashews to $1^1/_2$ cups, and add $1^1/_2$ cups water. The blueberry taste won't be as intense, but it will still be delicious.

Blueberry

$^1/_2$ cup chopped fresh organic blueberries, plus
22 ounces (about $4^1/_2$ cups) whole fresh organic blueberries
1 cup organic cashews or cashew pieces
1 cup maple syrup
1 tablespoon alcohol-free vanilla flavor
$^1/_8$ teaspoon alcohol-free almond flavor

MAKES ABOUT 1 QUART

Place the chopped blueberries in the freezer to chill.

Run the whole blueberries through a juicer to make 2 cups juice.

Combine the blueberry juice, cashews, syrup, vanilla flavor, and almond flavor in a blender. Blend on high until silky smooth, at least 1 minute. Place the blender in the freezer for 40 minutes to 1 hour or in the refrigerator for at least 1 hour or up to overnight, until well chilled. Pour the mixture into an

continued

ice cream maker and freeze according to the manufacturer's instructions. Remove the cover and blade from the ice cream maker and fold in the chopped blueberries, distributing evenly. Serve immediately or transfer to airtight containers and store in the freezer until ready to serve.

There is something seductive about velvety, fragrantly perfumed, ripe stone fruits. This ice cream captures some of the summery ambrosia of fresh peaches in a luxurious frozen treat. Garnish with slices of fresh ripe peaches.

Peach Nectar

2 pounds organic peaches, pitted
1 cup organic cashews or cashew pieces
1 cup maple syrup
1 tablespoon alcohol-free vanilla flavor
1/8 teaspoon alcohol-free almond flavor

MAKES ABOUT 1 QUART

Run the peaches through a juicer to make 2½ cups juice.

Combine the peach juice, cashews, syrup, vanilla flavor, and almond flavor in a blender. Blend on high until silky smooth, at least 1 minute.

Place the blender in the freezer for 40 minutes to 1 hour or in the refrigerator for at least 1 hour or up to overnight, until well chilled. Pour the mixture into an ice cream maker and freeze according to the manufacturer's instructions. Serve immediately or transfer to airtight containers and store in the freezer until ready to serve.

APRICOT NECTAR Replace the peaches with apricots.

Even on the coldest days, this delicate flavor may remind you of sun-drenched beaches and lush tropics. Garnish this sweet ice cream with fresh banana slices, dried banana chips, or shredded coconut.

Banana

1$\frac{1}{4}$ cups organic cashews or cashew pieces
2$\frac{1}{4}$ cups purified water
1 cup maple syrup
1 tablespoon alcohol-free vanilla flavor
1 cup mashed overripe organic banana (about 2 bananas)

MAKES ABOUT 1 QUART

Combine the cashews, water, syrup, and vanilla flavor in a blender. Blend on high until silky smooth, at least 1 minute. With the motor running, gradually add the banana and blend until smooth.

Place the blender in the freezer for 40 minutes to 1 hour or in the refrigerator for at least 1 hour or up to overnight, until well chilled. Pour the mixture into an ice cream maker and freeze according to the manufacturer's instructions. Serve immediately or transfer to airtight containers and store in the freezer until ready to serve.

This flavor offers a wonderful sweet-tart combination of vibrant fresh lemon and hearty, smooth maple syrup. The cashews bring them together into a splendid creamy texture.

Fresh Lemon

2 cups organic cashews or cashew pieces
1¼ cups purified water
1 cup maple syrup
¾ cup freshly squeezed lemon juice

MAKES ABOUT 1 QUART

Combine the cashews, water, syrup, and lemon juice in a blender. Blend on high until silky smooth, at least 1 minute.

Place the blender in the freezer for 40 minutes to 1 hour or in the refrigerator for at least 1 hour or up to overnight, until well chilled. Pour the mixture into an ice cream maker and freeze according to the manufacturer's instructions. Serve immediately or transfer to airtight containers and store in the freezer until ready to serve.

LEMON Increase the water to 2 cups and replace the lemon juice with 6 tablespoons alcohol-free lemon flavor.

There is a reason apple and cinnamon are a classic pair: bittersweet, earthy cinnamon dances beautifully with the crisp, sweet-tart flavors of apple on the taste buds. From mom's apple pie or apple strudel to hot spiced apple cider, apples and cinnamon enhance each other in a marriage made in the kitchen. Garnish this ice cream with chopped apples and cinnamon sticks.

Apple Cinnamon

3 cups bottled or fresh organic apple juice
1 cup organic cashews or cashew pieces
$^1/_2$ cup maple syrup
4 teaspoons freshly ground cinnamon

MAKES ABOUT 1 QUART

Combine the apple juice, cashews, syrup, and cinnamon in a blender. Blend on high until silky smooth, at least 1 minute.

Place the blender in the freezer for 40 minutes to 1 hour or in the refrigerator for at least 1 hour or up to overnight, until well chilled. Pour the mixture into an ice cream maker and freeze according to the manufacturer's instructions. Serve immediately or transfer to airtight containers and store in the freezer until ready to serve.

VEGAN ICE CREAM

The crisp, peppery gingersnap is one of my favorite cookies, and its signature notes of ginger and molasses transition very well into ice cream. The molasses offers a rich, hearty flavor. The ginger brings a bit of a spicy kick, and the cashews round out the flavor with a creamy mellowness. Garnish with a vegan almond, vanilla, or even gingersnap cookie.

Gingersnap

1³⁄₄ cups organic cashews or cashew pieces
1³⁄₄ cups purified water
1 cup maple syrup
6 to 8 teaspoons fresh organic ginger juice (see page 13)
3 tablespoons organic blackstrap molasses

MAKES ABOUT 1 QUART

Combine the cashews, water, syrup, 6 teaspoons ginger juice, and molasses in a blender. Blend on high until silky smooth, at least 1 minute. Taste the mixture and add up to 2 more teaspoons ginger juice to taste. Blend until evenly distributed.

Place the blender in the freezer for 40 minutes to 1 hour or in the refrigerator for at least 1 hour or up to overnight, until well chilled. Pour the mixture into an ice cream maker and freeze according to the manufacturer's instructions. Serve immediately or transfer to airtight containers and store in the freezer until ready to serve.

The clean, cooling flavor of peppermint is a winner in the hot summer months and mimics the frosty crispness of cold winter days as well. Mint is as at home in a refreshing julep sipped in humid temps as it is in candy canes and hot chocolate. The flavor similarly makes this ice cream a welcome treat all year-round. Garnish with a drizzle of Chocolate Sauce (page 120) and sprigs of fresh mint.

Peppermint

1³/₄ cups organic cashews or cashew pieces
1³/₄ cups purified water
1 cup maple syrup
2 teaspoons alcohol-free peppermint flavor
¹/₄ to ¹/₂ teaspoon spirulina powder (optional, see page 15)

MAKES ABOUT 1 QUART

Combine the cashews, water, syrup, peppermint flavor, and spirulina powder in a blender. Blend on high until silky smooth, at least 1 minute.

Place the blender in the freezer for 40 minutes to 1 hour or in the refrigerator for at least 1 hour or up to overnight, until well chilled. Pour the mixture into an ice cream maker and freeze according to the manufacturer's instructions. Serve immediately or transfer to airtight containers and store in the freezer until ready to serve.

My oldest brother had a taste for hot chiles, so prior to a trip to visit him and his family, I developed this recipe especially for him. The underlying flavor of jalapeño is fairly simple—fresh, vegetal, and pungent—yet it carries a wonderful heat. Just 1 teaspoon of minced jalapeño will give the ice cream a mild, crisp flavor with a little kick. Adding a second teaspoon will give you more heat, and 3 teaspoons will deliver quite a punch. Start with a small amount and add more chile to taste.

Jalapeño Heaven

1 to 3 teaspoons minced organic jalapeño
2 cups organic cashews or cashew pieces
2 cups purified water
1 cup maple syrup

MAKES ABOUT 1 QUART

Combine the jalapeño, cashews, water, and syrup in a blender. Blend on high until silky smooth, at least 1 minute.

Place the blender in the freezer for 40 minutes to 1 hour or in the refrigerator for at least 1 hour or up to overnight, until well chilled. Pour the mixture into an ice cream maker and freeze according to the manufacturer's instructions. Serve immediately or transfer to airtight containers and store in the freezer until ready to serve.

Black Forest torte is a German dessert in which layers of sour cherries offer a tangy complement to kirsch-soaked chocolate cake. I re-create this exquisite combination in an ice cream. My favorite cherry variety is Lambert, through Bing and other dark cherries offer a similar flavor. Rainer cherries are much lighter and more colorful and offer a brighter flavor.

Black Forest

1³⁄₄ pounds organic Lambert, Bing, or Rainier cherries, pitted, plus 1 cup chopped pitted cherries
1 cup organic cashews or cashew pieces
³⁄₄ cup maple syrup
¹⁄₄ teaspoon alcohol-free almond flavor
¹⁄₂ cup unsweetened cocoa powder

MAKES ABOUT 1 QUART

Run the 1¾ pounds cherries through a juicer to make 2 cups juice. Place the chopped cherries in the freezer to chill.

Combine the cherry juice, cashews, syrup, and almond flavor in a blender. Blend on high until silky smooth, at least 1 minute. With the motor running, add the cocoa powder and blend until evenly distributed.

Place the blender in the freezer for 40 minutes to 1 hour or in the refrigerator for at least 1 hour or up to overnight, until well chilled. Pour the cherry juice mixture into an ice cream maker and freeze according to the manufacturer's instructions. Remove the cover and blade from the ice cream maker and fold in the chopped cherries, distributing evenly. Serve immediately or transfer to airtight containers and store in the freezer until ready to serve.

If using fresh pumpkin, I recommend a Sugar Pie pumpkin. Cut it in half, removing the stem and seeds. Cut into 2-inch slices and steam until tender. Scrape the flesh away from the skin, and it is ready to use. Garnish the finished ice cream with a vegan whipped cream topping or chopped toasted pumpkin seeds.

Pumpkin

1 cup organic cashews or cashew pieces
1½ cups purified water
1 cup maple syrup
2 tablespoons alcohol-free vanilla flavor
¼ teaspoon alcohol-free almond flavor
3 tablespoons minced fresh organic ginger
1½ teaspoons ground nutmeg
½ teaspoon ground cloves
½ teaspoon ground cinnamon
¼ teaspoon ground allspice
1 cup cooked organic pumpkin or canned organic pumpkin puree

MAKES ABOUT 1 QUART

Combine the cashews, water, syrup, vanilla flavor, almond flavor, ginger, nutmeg, cloves, cinnamon, and allspice in a blender. Blend on high until silky smooth, at least 1 minute. With the motor running, add the pumpkin and blend until creamy.

Place the blender in the freezer for 40 minutes to 1 hour or in the refrigerator for at least 1 hour or up to overnight, until well chilled. Pour the mixture into an ice cream maker and freeze according to the manufacturer's instructions. Serve immediately or transfer to airtight containers and store in the freezer until ready to serve.

Carrot cake has long been viewed as a health-conscious dessert choice, thanks to the healthful properties of carrots and their high vitamin content. But the natural sugars and moisture of carrots also lend them well to soft, delicious cakes, and even as a youth, I had a hard time choosing between carrot cake and chocolate cake from restaurant dessert menus. I've captured the mildly spiced, crisp-sweet flavors of that luscious cake in this wonderful ice cream. Garnish with a vegan whipped cream topping and chopped walnuts.

Carrot Cake

$^1/_2$ cup chopped organic walnuts

$2^1/_2$ pounds organic carrots

2 cups organic cashews or cashew pieces

1 cup maple syrup

1 teaspoon alcohol-free vanilla flavor

$^1/_4$ teaspoon alcohol-free almond flavor

2 teaspoons ground cinnamon

2 teaspoons ground nutmeg

$^1/_4$ teaspoon ground cloves

$^1/_8$ teaspoon ground allspice

MAKES ABOUT 1 QUART

Place the walnuts in the freezer to chill.

Run the carrots through a juicer to make 2 cups juice. (You can also puree the carrots in a blender and then pass them through a fine-mesh bag and squeeze the juice out.)

Combine the carrot juice, cashews, syrup, vanilla flavor, almond flavor, cinnamon, nutmeg, cloves, and allspice in a blender. Blend on high until silky smooth, at least 1 minute.

Place the blender in the freezer for 40 minutes to 1 hour or in the refrigerator for at least 1 hour or up to overnight, until well chilled. Pour the mixture into an ice cream maker and freeze according to the manufacturer's instructions. Remove the cover and blade from the ice cream maker and fold in the walnuts, distributing evenly. Serve immediately or transfer to airtight containers and store in the freezer until ready to serve.

RAW
ICE CREAM

Make this bright-tasting ice cream during the summer months to take advantage of the abundance of juicy, luscious strawberries at their peak. For some added texture and color, chop several strawberries and freeze for at least 15 minutes, then mix them into the finished ice cream. Garnish with strawberry slices.

Raw Strawberry

1 vanilla bean, sliced and scraped
1½ cups almond milk (page 13)
1½ cups packed hulled organic strawberries
1 cup packed organic pitted honey dates (see page 7)

MAKES ABOUT 1 QUART

Combine the scraped vanilla bean seeds, almond milk, and strawberries in a blender. Blend until smooth. With the motor running, gradually add the dates and blend on high until silky smooth, at least 1 minute.

Place the blender in the freezer for 40 minutes to 1 hour or in the refrigerator for at least 1 hour or up to overnight, until well chilled. Pour the mixture into an ice cream maker and freeze according to the manufacturer's instructions. Serve immediately or transfer to airtight containers and store in the freezer until ready to serve.

In this refreshing version of strawberry ice cream, coconut water adds a mild sweetness, while the cashews offer a lovely creamy texture without the work involved with other nut milks. Garnish the finished ice cream with strawberry slices.

Raw Strawberry Too

1¼ pounds fresh organic strawberries, hulled
1 cup young coconut water (see page 11)
½ cup raw organic cashews or cashew pieces
¾ cup packed organic pitted honey dates (see page 7)

MAKES ABOUT 1 QUART

Run the strawberries through a juicer to make 2 cups juice.

Combine the coconut water and cashews in a blender. Blend until smooth. With the motor running, gradually add the strawberry juice and dates and blend on high until silky smooth, at least 1 minute.

Place the blender in the freezer for 40 minutes to 1 hour or in the refrigerator for at least 1 hour or up to overnight, until well chilled. Pour the mixture into an ice cream maker and freeze according to the manufacturer's instructions. Serve immediately or transfer to airtight containers and store in the freezer until ready to serve.

Far from mom's strawberry rhubarb pie, this recipe is not only vegan, but it is also raw! The long season of mid- to late spring to early autumn offers plenty of time to take advantage of the wonderful tartness of fresh rhubarb. The leaves of the plant are toxic, so use only the stalks for eating.

Raw Strawberry Rhubarb

22 ounces organic rhubarb (about 8 stalks)
$^1/_2$ cup raw organic cashews or cashew pieces
1 cup packed organic pitted honey dates (see page 7)
1 cup packed hulled organic strawberries

MAKES ABOUT 1 QUART

Run the rhubarb through a juicer to make 2 cups juice.

Combine the rhubarb juice and cashews in a blender. Blend until smooth. With the motor running, gradually add the dates and blend on high until silky smooth, at least 1 minute. Add the strawberries and blend until smooth.

Place the blender in the freezer for 40 minutes to 1 hour or in the refrigerator for at least 1 hour or up to overnight, until well chilled. Pour the mixture into an ice cream maker and freeze according to the manufacturer's instructions. Serve immediately or transfer to airtight containers and store in the freezer until ready to serve.

I have long been a fan of piña coladas. The tropical blend of golden, tangy pineapple and creamy coconut milk tastes wonderful to me. This variation adds the refreshing flavor of fresh strawberries. Be sure to use fresh coconut milk, as it will add more flavorful magic to the recipe than traditional canned or frozen coconut milk. Garnish with a slice of pineapple placed on the rim of the serving dish.

Strawberry Colada

1³/₄ pounds organic Sugar Loaf pineapple,
peeled and cut into 1-inch chunks
14 ounces fresh organic strawberries, hulled
1¹/₂ cups fresh coconut milk (see page 9)
³/₄ cup packed organic pitted honey dates (see page 7),
plus more as needed

MAKES ABOUT 1 QUART

Run the pineapple through a juicer to make 1½ cups juice. Run the strawberries through a juicer to make 1 cup juice.

Combine the pineapple juice, strawberry juice, and coconut milk in a blender. With the motor running, gradually add the dates, tasting occasionally. When the mixture has achieved the desired sweetness, stop adding the dates and blend on high until silky smooth, at least 1 minute.

Place the blender in the freezer for 40 minutes to 1 hour or in the refrigerator for at least 1 hour or up to overnight, until well chilled. Pour the mixture into an ice cream maker and freeze according to the manufacturer's instructions. Serve immediately or transfer to airtight containers and store in the freezer until ready to serve.

I came up with this combination while in the produce section of our local health food store. Brilliant, sweet-tart kiwis were stacked adjacent to succulent, tangy mandarin oranges, and it sounded like a magical pair. A new flavor was born! The kiwis should give slightly to the touch, otherwise they will be tart and you will need more sweetener. If you cannot find mandarins, use tangerines. Otherwise, use Valencia or other oranges. Each variety of citrus will offer its own unique flavor. Garnish with a slice of kiwi or orange, placed over the rim of the serving dish, and a few pomegranate seeds, if desired.

Kiwi Mandarin

2 pounds organic Delite mandarin oranges, peeled and seeded
1^3/$_4$ pounds organic kiwis, peeled
^{1}/$_2$ cup packed organic pitted honey dates (see page 7)

MAKES ABOUT 1 QUART

Run the mandarins through a juicer to make 1¾ cups juice. Run the kiwis through a juicer to make 1¾ cups juice.

Combine the mandarin juice and kiwi juice in a blender. With the motor running, gradually add the dates. Blend on high until silky smooth, at least 1 minute.

Place the blender in the freezer for 40 minutes to 1 hour or in the refrigerator for at least 1 hour or up to overnight, until well chilled. Pour the mixture into an ice cream maker and freeze according to the manufacturer's instructions. Serve immediately or transfer to airtight containers and store in the freezer until ready to serve.

This combination offers a juicy, sweet-tart tropical flavor. As citrus fruits may vary in flavor and sweetness, be sure to sweeten to taste. If you cannot find mandarins, use tangerines. Otherwise, use Valencia or other oranges. Garnish with peeled sections of mandarin.

Mandarin Grapefruit

2 pounds organic mandarin oranges, peeled
1 organic grapefruit, peeled
1¼ cups mashed overripe organic banana (about 2½ bananas)
¼ cup raw organic agave nectar

MAKES ABOUT 1 QUART

Run the mandarins through a juicer to make 2 cups juice. Run the grapefruit through a juicer to make ½ cup juice.

Combine the mandarin juice, grapefruit juice, banana, and agave nectar in a blender. Blend on high until silky smooth, at least 1 minute.

Place the blender in the freezer for 40 minutes to 1 hour or in the refrigerator for at least 1 hour or up to overnight, until well chilled. Pour the mixture into an ice cream maker and freeze according to the manufacturer's instructions. Serve immediately or transfer to airtight containers and store in the freezer until ready to serve.

I look forward to nectarine season all year—they are my favorite of the stone fruits. There is something incredibly satisfying about a delicious, fragrantly perfumed nectarine. To pick the best nectarines, like peaches, look for rich colors, floral aromas, and a firm texture that gives slightly to the touch. Garnish your ice cream with chopped nectarines.

Nectarine

2 cups almond milk (page 13)
1/2 cup packed organic pitted Medjool dates (see page 7)
1 1/2 cups peeled, pitted, and sliced organic nectarines

MAKES ABOUT 1 QUART

Put the almond milk in a blender. With the motor running, gradually add the dates. Blend on high until silky smooth, at least 1 minute. With the motor running, gradually add the nectarines and blend until smooth.

Place the blender in the freezer for 40 minutes to 1 hour or in the refrigerator for at least 1 hour or up to overnight, until well chilled. Pour the mixture into an ice cream maker and freeze according to the manufacturer's instructions. Serve immediately or transfer to airtight containers and store in the freezer until ready to serve.

Make this subtle and cooling ice cream in the summer to take advantage of succulent, aromatic melons when they're at their peak. While the most popular melons may be watermelon, honeydew, and cantaloupe, feel free to experiment and try any variety you find when exploring the farmers' market. The sweetness of melons varies, so be sure to sweeten to taste.

Melon Mania

2½ pounds sliced organic honeydew melon or cantaloupe
1 cup raw organic cashews or cashew pieces
½ cup packed organic pitted Medjool dates (see page 7)

MAKES ABOUT 1 QUART

Run the melon through a juicer to make 3 cups juice.

Combine the melon juice and cashews in a blender. Blend until smooth. With the motor running, gradually add the dates and blend on high until silky smooth, at least 1 minute.

Place the blender in the freezer for 40 minutes to 1 hour or in the refrigerator for at least 1 hour or up to overnight, until well chilled. Pour the mixture into an ice cream maker and freeze according to the manufacturer's instructions. Serve immediately or transfer to airtight containers and store in the freezer until ready to serve.

This bright and fresh flavor wakes up the taste buds and instantly calls to mind childhood mornings drinking Concord grape juice along with breakfast. The creamy texture and flavor of cashews provides a subtle backdrop to the fruity burst of grape.

Concord Grape

2¼ pounds organic Concord grapes
1 cup raw organic cashews or cashew pieces
½ cup packed organic pitted honey dates (see page 7)

MAKES ABOUT 1 QUART

Run the grapes through a juicer to make 3 cups juice.

Combine the grape juice and cashews in a blender. Blend until smooth. With the motor running, gradually add the dates and blend on high until silky smooth, at least 1 minute.

Place the blender in the freezer for 40 minutes to 1 hour or in the refrigerator for at least 1 hour or up to overnight, until well chilled. Pour the mixture into an ice cream maker and freeze according to the manufacturer's instructions. Serve immediately or transfer to airtight containers and store in the freezer until ready to serve.

This jewel-like, scarlet fruit has a tart, warming flavor we associate with Thanksgiving and other winter holidays. Make this ice cream at the end of the year when cranberries are plentiful and when cooling autumn days call for a jolt of color and robust flavor. Sweeten the recipe to satisfy your own taste buds.

Cranberry

1½ cups fresh organic cranberries
2 cups purified water
½ cup packed organic pitted honey dates (see page 7)
1 cup mashed overripe organic banana

MAKES ABOUT 1 QUART

Combine the cranberries and water in a blender. Blend on high until very smooth, at least 1 minute. With the motor running, gradually add the dates and blend until silky smooth. With the motor running, gradually add the banana and blend until creamy.

Place the blender in the freezer for 40 minutes to 1 hour or in the refrigerator for at least 1 hour or up to overnight, until well chilled. Pour the mixture into an ice cream maker and freeze according to the manufacturer's instructions. Serve immediately or transfer to airtight containers and store in the freezer until ready to serve.

I love stone fruit season, and while succulent nectarines are my favorite, luscious, velvety peaches are a close second. In this ice cream, the natural sweetness of coconut water and dates allow the floral notes and summery punch of peaches to shine. To pick the best peaches, look for rich colors, intense fragrance, and texture that gives slightly to the touch. Garnish your ice cream with chopped peaches.

Peach

1½ cups coconut water (see page 11)
½ cup raw organic cashews or cashew pieces
2 cups packed sliced organic peaches
½ cup packed organic pitted honey dates (see page 7)

MAKES ABOUT 1 QUART

Combine the coconut water and cashews in a blender. Blend until smooth. With the motor running, gradually add the peaches and dates and blend on high until silky smooth, at least 1 minute.

Place the blender in the freezer for 40 minutes to 1 hour or in the refrigerator for at least 1 hour or up to overnight, until well chilled. Pour the mixture into an ice cream maker and freeze according to the manufacturer's instructions. Serve immediately or transfer to airtight containers and store in the freezer until ready to serve.

What can I say? I had to try it! The combination of bright, juicy blueberries with creamy, floral peaches is amazing. Blueberries are a nutritional powerhouse; if you're using organic fruit, I recommend leaving the peaches unpeeled to retain the nutrients found in the skin.

Blueberry Peach

24 ounces (about 5 cups) organic blueberries
1³/₄ pounds organic peaches, pitted
³/₄ cup packed organic pitted honey dates (see page 7)

MAKES 1 QUART

Run the blueberries through a juicer to make 1¾ cups juice. Run the peaches through a juicer to make 1¾ cups juice.

Combine the blueberry juice and peach juice in a blender. With the motor running, gradually add the dates. Blend on high until silky smooth, at least 1 minute.

Place the blender in the freezer for 40 minutes to 1 hour or in the refrigerator for at least 1 hour or up to overnight, until well chilled. Pour the mixture into an ice cream maker and freeze according to the manufacturer's instructions. Serve immediately or transfer to airtight containers and store in the freezer until ready to serve.

The name of this ice cream alone almost makes me drool!
There is something decadent about apple strudel. It's a heaven-
sent taste sensation! Somehow I managed to capture the crisp,
golden-brown magic of the baked dessert in this recipe.
The coconut milk really does the trick, providing a rich
counterbalance to the sweet fruit and crunchy pecans.
Garnish with soaked raisins and chopped nuts.

Apple Strudel

1 cup raisins
1¼ pounds organic Fuji apples, plus 1 cup chopped apple
1 cup fresh coconut milk (see page 9)
1 tablespoon freshly ground cinnamon
1 cup chopped organic pecans

MAKES ABOUT 1 QUART

Place the raisins in a jar and add enough water to cover.
Refrigerate overnight. Drain, reserving the sweet soaking
liquid. (To add extra sweetness, you may want to use the
soaking liquid in place of some of the coconut water, or you
can save it for another use.)

Run the 1¼ pounds apples through a juicer to make
1½ cups juice.

Combine the apple juice, coconut milk, and cinnamon in
a blender. Blend on high until silky smooth, at least 1 minute.
Place the blender in the freezer for 40 minutes to 1 hour or in
the refrigerator for at least 1 hour or up to overnight, until
well chilled.

Place the chopped apple, raisins, and pecans in the freezer to chill.

Pour the apple juice mixture into an ice cream maker and freeze according to the manufacturer's instructions. Remove the cover and blade from the ice cream maker and fold in the chopped apples, raisins, and pecans, distributing evenly. Serve immediately or transfer to airtight containers and store in the freezer until ready to serve.

For citrus lovers or fans of sweet-and-sour desserts, this is a delightful and refreshing flavor. This recipe is also naturally low in fat, so those watching their fat intake can indulge!

Banana Lemon

2$\frac{1}{2}$ pounds organic lemons
$\frac{1}{2}$ cup packed organic pitted Medjool dates (see page 7)
1 cup mashed slightly overripe organic banana (about 2 bananas)
$\frac{1}{2}$ cup purified water

MAKES ABOUT 1 QUART

Peel the lemons. Separate into sections and remove the membrane and seeds from each section. You should have 2 cups lemon segments.

Put the lemon segments in a blender. With the motor running, gradually add the dates and blend on high until creamy, at least 1 minute. Add the banana and continue blending until creamy. Add enough of the water to make 4 cups total and blend until thoroughly mixed.

Place the blender in the freezer for 40 minutes to 1 hour or in the refrigerator for at least 1 hour or up to overnight, until well chilled. Pour the mixture into an ice cream maker and freeze according to the manufacturer's instructions. Serve immediately or transfer to airtight containers and store in the freezer until ready to serve.

It's amazing what one can make with only two ingredients!
The delicate, tropical flavors of banana play beautifully against
the succulent high notes of the cherries. Naturally low in fat
but high in flavor and nutrition, this recipe is very satisfying
and perfect for enjoying on a hot summer afternoon.
Garnish with pitted and halved cherries.

Banana Cherry

2 cups mashed overripe organic bananas (about 4 bananas)
2 cups packed organic pitted Bing, Lambert, or Rainier cherries

MAKES ABOUT 1 QUART

Combine the bananas and 1 cup of the cherries in a food processor fitted with the metal blade. Process until silky smooth, at
least 1 minute. Place the food processor bowl in the freezer for
40 minutes to 1 hour or in the refrigerator for at least 1 hour or
up to overnight, until well chilled.

Chop the remaining 1 cup cherries and place in the freezer
to chill.

Pour the banana-cherry mixture into an ice cream maker
and freeze according to the manufacturer's instructions. Remove
the cover and blade from the ice cream maker and fold in the
chopped cherries, distributing evenly. Serve immediately or
transfer to airtight containers and store in the freezer until
ready to serve.

Nutritious, juicy blueberries and delicately sweet bananas balance to make a well-rounded, refreshing treat. The fresh coconut milk offers an amazing creaminess as well as flavor to marry the fruit. The fresh vanilla enhances the experience.

Banana Blueberry

1^1/$_2$ cups organic blueberries
1^1/$_4$ cups mashed overripe organic bananas (about 2^1/$_2$ bananas)
1 cup fresh coconut milk (see page 9)
^{1}/$_2$ cup raw organic agave nectar
1 vanilla bean, sliced and scraped (see page 15)

MAKES ABOUT 1 QUART

Combine the blueberries, bananas, coconut milk, agave nectar, and scraped vanilla bean seeds in a blender. Blend on high until silky smooth, at least 1 minute.

Place the blender in the freezer for 40 minutes to 1 hour or in the refrigerator for at least 1 hour or up to overnight, until well chilled. Pour the mixture into an ice cream maker and freeze according to the manufacturer's instructions. Serve immediately or transfer to airtight containers and store in the freezer until ready to serve.

Figs are an amazing fruit. Their season—late summer—comes and goes too quickly for me, so seize the moment when they're at their peak and extend your enjoyment of them in this elegant ice cream! Ripe figs should give slightly to pressure and be sweet smelling. Use the best and ripest you have available. Try different varieties for changes in flavor. In recent years, I've discovered Adriatic figs. When ripe, the center is an amazing red and the flavor is reminiscent of strawberry jam.

Fig

2 cups fresh coconut milk (see page 9)
1 1/2 cups peeled fresh figs
3/4 cup packed organic pitted honey dates (see page 7)

MAKES ABOUT 1 QUART

Combine the coconut milk and figs in a blender. Blend until smooth. With the motor running, gradually add the dates and blend on high until silky smooth, at least 1 minute.

Place the blender in the freezer for 40 minutes to 1 hour or in the refrigerator for at least 1 hour or up to overnight, until well chilled. Pour the mixture into an ice cream maker and freeze according to the manufacturer's instructions. Serve immediately or transfer to airtight containers and store in the freezer until ready to serve.

Durian is a fascinating fruit. It is amazing to some, who revere it as the "king of fruits." However, it's also called "stinky fruit," and many find it repellant. The only way to find out whether you have the taste buds for this fruit is to try it. I'm a big fan. The best durian is luxurious and tastes like a honey pudding. Fresh coconut milk is its perfect partner, as it smoothes out the flavor and texture of durian and offers a little tropical magic.

Coconut Durian

2 cups fresh coconut milk (see page 9), plus more as needed
1¼ cups peeled and seeded durian (see page 12)
(about 2½ pounds durian)
¼ cup packed organic pitted honey dates (see page 7)

MAKES ABOUT 1 QUART

Combine the coconut milk and durian in a blender. Blend until smooth. With the motor running, gradually add the dates and blend on high until silky smooth, at least 1 minute. If the mixture seems too thick and is difficult to blend, add more coconut milk. Blend again until smooth.

Place the blender in the freezer for 40 minutes to 1 hour or in the refrigerator for at least 1 hour or up to overnight, until well chilled. Pour the mixture into an ice cream maker and freeze according to the manufacturer's instructions. Serve immediately or transfer to airtight containers and store in the freezer until ready to serve.

This is one of the most amazing chocolate flavors I've come up with. Of course, that is coming from a durian fan. Sweet, milky coconut and creamy, custardlike durian are already a wonderful combination—the cacao just makes the ice cream dance on the taste buds.

Coconut Cacao Durian

1¹/₂ cups fresh coconut milk (see page 9), plus more as needed
1 pound peeled and seeded durian (see page 12)
(about 3¹/₂ pounds durian)
1 vanilla bean, split and scraped (see page 15)
¹/₂ cup raw organic cacao powder
1 organic apricot kernel (see page 8)

MAKES ABOUT 1 QUART

Combine the coconut milk, durian, scraped vanilla bean seeds, cacao powder, and apricot kernel in a blender. Blend on high until silky smooth, at least 1 minute.

Place the blender in the freezer for 40 minutes to 1 hour or in the refrigerator for at least 1 hour or up to overnight, until well chilled. Pour the mixture into an ice cream maker and freeze according to the manufacturer's instructions. Serve immediately or transfer to airtight containers and store in the freezer until ready to serve.

As a durian fan, I find this flavor combination to be such a sensual experience. The mix of creamy coconut, slightly sweet durian, and juicy strawberry is soothing and delightful. It is almost intoxicating.

Coconut Strawberry Durian

2 cups packed hulled organic strawberries
1 cup fresh coconut milk (see page 9)
1 cup peeled and seeded durian (see page 12)
$^{1}/_{4}$ cup organic agave nectar
1 vanilla bean, split and scraped (see page 15)
1 organic apricot kernel (see page 8)

MAKES ABOUT 1 QUART

Combine the strawberries, coconut milk, durian, agave nectar, scraped vanilla bean seeds, and apricot kernel in a blender. Blend on high until silky smooth, at least 1 minute.

Place the blender in the freezer for 40 minutes to 1 hour or in the refrigerator for at least 1 hour or up to overnight, until well chilled. Pour the mixture into an ice cream maker and freeze according to the manufacturer's instructions. Serve immediately or transfer to airtight containers and store in the freezer until ready to serve.

The real heroes of the recipes in this chapter come from nature, and this flavor is a prime example of how a simple trio of ingredients can come together effortlessly. Fresh coconut milk is an amazing base for ice creams, and, in this case, marries with the flavor of rich ripe cherries. Dates delicately sweeten the pair. Garnish the ice cream with pitted and halved cherries.

Coconut Cherry

2 cups fresh coconut milk (see page 9), plus more as needed
2 cups packed organic pitted Bing, Lambert, or Rainier cherries
$^1/_2$ cup packed organic pitted honey dates (see page 7)

MAKES ABOUT 1 QUART

Combine the coconut milk and cherries in a blender. Blend until smooth. With the motor running, gradually add the dates and blend on high until silky smooth, at least 1 minute. If the mixture seems too thick and is difficult to blend, add more coconut milk. Blend again until smooth.

Place the blender in the freezer for 40 minutes to 1 hour or in the refrigerator for at least 1 hour or up to overnight, until well chilled. Pour the mixture into an ice cream maker and freeze according to the manufacturer's instructions. Serve immediately or transfer to airtight containers and store in the freezer until ready to serve.

The small number of ingredients in this recipe in no way represents how big the flavor is! The heavenly essence of the coconut merges with the bright, fruity tang of the strawberries to fully please the senses.

Coconut Strawberry

2 cups fresh coconut milk (see page 9), plus more as needed
1¼ cups packed hulled organic strawberries
¾ cup packed organic pitted honey dates (see page 7)

MAKES ABOUT 1 QUART

Combine the coconut milk and strawberries in a blender. Blend until smooth. With the motor running, gradually add the dates and blend on high until silky smooth, at least 1 minute. If the mixture seems too thick and is difficult to blend, add more coconut milk. Blend again until smooth.

Place the blender in the freezer for 40 minutes to 1 hour or in the refrigerator for at least 1 hour or up to overnight, until well chilled. Pour the mixture into an ice cream maker and freeze according to the manufacturer's instructions. Serve immediately or transfer to airtight containers and store in the freezer until ready to serve.

This recipe doesn't just speak, it sings of the tropics. Mango, in and of itself, is delectable and intoxicatingly tangy-sweet, but when paired with coconut, magic happens! This is a delightful flavor that may have you visualizing palm trees and white sand beaches.

Coconut Mango

4 pounds fresh mangoes, peeled and pitted
1¼ cups fresh coconut milk (see page 9)
¾ cup packed organic pitted honey dates (see page 7), plus more as needed

MAKES ABOUT 1 QUART

Run the mangoes through a juicer to make 3 cups juice.

Combine the mango juice and coconut milk in a blender. With the motor running, gradually add the dates, tasting occasionally. When the mixture has achieved the desired sweetness, stop adding the dates and blend on high until silky smooth, at least 1 minute.

Place the blender in the freezer for 40 minutes to 1 hour or in the refrigerator for at least 1 hour or up to overnight, until well chilled. Pour the mixture into an ice cream maker and freeze according to the manufacturer's instructions. Serve immediately or transfer to airtight containers and store in the freezer until ready to serve.

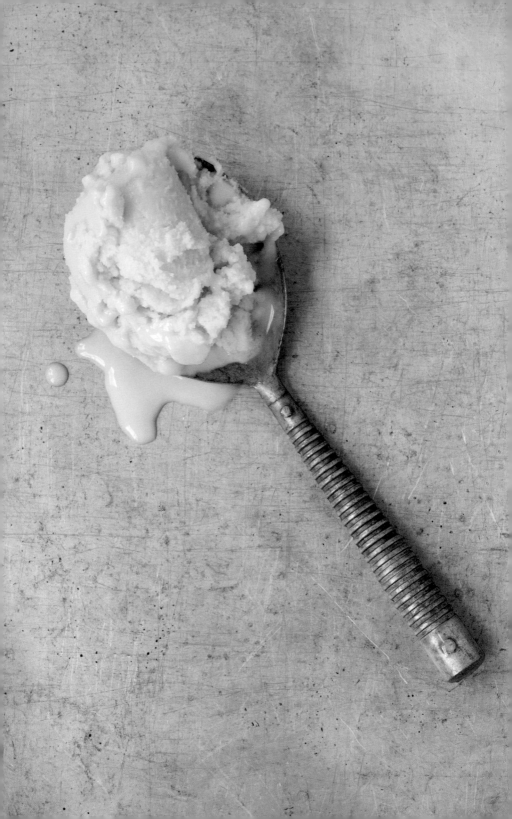

Another lovely tropical flavor, this combination calls to mind a cheery mango piña colada. Bright-tasting, juicy mangoes and pineapple are cradled by the creamy flavor of coconut milk. This ice cream is a beautiful, vibrant gold. All that's missing is the tiny paper umbrella.

Pineapple Mango

2 large organic mangoes, peeled and pitted
1 organic pineapple, skinned and cut into 1-inch chunks
1 cup fresh coconut milk (see page 9)
$1/2$ cup raw organic agave nectar

MAKES ABOUT 1 QUART

Run the mangoes through a juicer to make $1^{1}/_{4}$ cups juice. Run the pineapple through a juicer to make $1^{1}/_{4}$ cups juice.

Combine the mango juice, pineapple juice, coconut milk, and agave nectar in a blender. Blend on high until silky smooth, at least 1 minute.

Place the blender in the freezer for 40 minutes to 1 hour or in the refrigerator for at least 1 hour or up to overnight, until well chilled. Pour the mixture into an ice cream maker and freeze according to the manufacturer's instructions. Serve immediately or transfer to airtight containers and store in the freezer until ready to serve.

"Put the lime in the coconut," as the song goes. Very cooling and sensual, this unique flavor combination blends coconut milk, ginger, and kaffir lime leaves to create a tropical flavor that diverts your thoughts to the Caribbean. Look for the lime leaves in the chilled herb section of grocery stores and Asian markets.

Coconut Lime Leaf Ginger

3¼ cups fresh coconut milk (see page 9)
1 tablespoon fresh organic ginger juice (see page 13)
11 medium kaffir lime leaves, rinsed
¾ cup packed organic pitted honey dates (see page 7)

MAKES ABOUT 1 QUART

Combine the coconut milk, ginger juice, and lime leaves in a blender. Blend until smooth. With the motor running, gradually add the dates and blend on high until silky smooth, at least 1 minute.

Place the blender in the freezer for 40 minutes to 1 hour or in the refrigerator for at least 1 hour or up to overnight, until well chilled. Pour the mixture into an ice cream maker and freeze according to the manufacturer's instructions. Serve immediately or transfer to airtight containers and store in the freezer until ready to serve.

I first experienced the surprising combination of coconut and avocado in a smoothie when I was living in Hawaii. Many people suffer from various nut allergies, so this recipe makes use of creamy avocado, rather than nuts, as an ice cream base. Here, buttery, lush avocado is paired, very pleasantly, with coconut milk. A ripe avocado should give slightly to the touch.

Coconut Avocado

2^1/$_2$ cups fresh coconut milk (see page 9)
1 cup mashed organic avocado (about 1^1/$_2$ avocados)
^{1}/$_2$ cup raw organic agave nectar
1 tablespoon ground cinnamon

MAKES ABOUT 1 QUART

Combine the coconut milk, avocado, agave nectar, and cinnamon in a blender. Blend on high until silky smooth, at least 1 minute.

Place the blender in the freezer for 40 minutes to 1 hour or in the refrigerator for at least 1 hour or up to overnight, until well chilled. Pour the mixture into an ice cream maker and freeze according to the manufacturer's instructions. Serve immediately or transfer to airtight containers and store in the freezer until ready to serve.

I first used this combination when I looked in my refrigerator one morning for something to eat. All I had were some red flame grapes (red seedless table grapes) and an avocado on my counter. Neither one was especially appetizing at that moment. Then I had an epiphany. I blended the two to create a surprisingly delicious pudding. Here I have adapted that recipe to create a remarkable ice cream.

Avocado Grape

1 cup mashed organic avocado (about 1½ avocados)
3 cups organic red flame grapes

MAKES ABOUT 1 QUART

Combine the avocado and grapes in a blender. Blend on high until silky smooth, at least 1 minute.

Place the blender in the freezer for 40 minutes to 1 hour or in the refrigerator for at least 1 hour or up to overnight, until well chilled. Pour the mixture into an ice cream maker and freeze according to the manufacturer's instructions. Serve immediately or transfer to airtight containers and store in the freezer until ready to serve.

AVOCADO GRAPE GINGER Add 1 to 3 teaspoons fresh organic ginger juice (see page 13).

In my college days, I made the best piña coladas on campus (IMO)! I started leaving out the rum a long time ago, but I still love the tropical flavor combination of coconut and pineapple. I find it almost enchanting. While Sugar Loaf may be optimal, use the best fresh pineapple you can find. A ripe pineapple should be slightly soft when squeezed and should be sweet smelling.

Piña Colada

2¼ pounds organic Sugar Loaf pineapple, cut into 1-inch chunks
1 cup packed organic pitted honey dates (see page 7)
2 cups fresh coconut milk (see page 9)

MAKES ABOUT 1 QUART

Run the pineapple through a juicer to make 2 cups juice.

Put the pineapple juice in a blender. With the motor running, gradually add the dates and blend on high until silky smooth, at least 1 minute. If the mixture seems too thick and is difficult to blend, add a little of the coconut milk and blend until smooth. Add the remaining coconut milk and blend again until smooth.

Place the blender in the freezer for 40 minutes to 1 hour or in the refrigerator for at least 1 hour or up to overnight, until well chilled. Pour the mixture into an ice cream maker and freeze according to the manufacturer's instructions. Serve immediately or transfer to airtight containers and store in the freezer until ready to serve.

Pomegranates are an ancient fruit that produce a rich sweet juice with a gorgeous red color. To remove the seeds, score the skin of the fruit with a knife to make four or more sections. Pull the sections apart. While holding a section, skin side up, over a deep bowl or pot, hit the skin repeatedly with a wooden dowel or the handle of a kitchen utensil. Continue until all of the seeds are out of each section.

Pomegranate

Seeds from 4 large organic pomegranates
1 cup soaked raw organic cashews or cashew pieces
$1/2$ cup raw organic agave nectar
2 tablespoons raw organic coconut oil

MAKES ABOUT 1 QUART

Run the pomegranate seeds through a food mill to make $3^{1}/_{4}$ cups pomegranate juice.

Combine the pomegranate juice, cashews, agave nectar, and coconut oil in a blender. Blend on high until silky smooth, at least 1 minute.

Place the blender in the freezer for 40 minutes to 1 hour or in the refrigerator for at least 1 hour or up to overnight, until well chilled. Pour the mixture into an ice cream maker and freeze according to the manufacturer's instructions. Serve immediately or transfer to airtight containers and store in the freezer until ready to serve.

Pomegranate juice brings a brilliant scarlet color and a magical flavor to the piña colada. The refreshing juice of the pomegranate perfectly complements the coconut milk and pineapple juice while smoothing all of the flavors together. Garnish this ice cream with some pomegranate seeds.

Pomegranate Colada

Seeds from 2 large organic pomegranates
1 organic pineapple, skinned and cut into 1-inch chunks
1 cup fresh coconut milk (see page 9)
$^1/_2$ cup raw organic agave nectar

MAKES ABOUT 1 QUART

Run the pomegranate seeds through a food mill to make $1^1/_4$ cups pomegranate juice. Run the pineapple through a juicer to make $1^1/_4$ cups juice.

Combine the pomegranate juice, pineapple juice, coconut milk, and agave nectar in a blender. Blend on high until silky smooth, at least 1 minute.

Place the blender in the freezer for 40 minutes to 1 hour or in the refrigerator for at least 1 hour or up to overnight, until well chilled. Pour the mixture into an ice cream maker and freeze according to the manufacturer's instructions. Serve immediately or transfer to airtight containers and store in the freezer until ready to serve.

While many of my friends stuck to standard chocolate or vanilla flavors, I equally enjoyed pistachio ice cream as a child. When the first edition of this book was published, I had not created a recipe worthy of the book. But now I have perfected a version I love, in which coconut milk, agave nectar, and vanilla form a supporting cast of sweetness to round out the subtle flavor of the nuts. A fun variation (pictured opposite) is to pack some finished vegan ice cream between your favorite chilled cookies, roll the edge in chopped pistachios, refreeze to firm, and then enjoy!

Pistachio Coconut

1³/₄ cups pistachio milk (page 14)
1³/₄ cups fresh coconut milk (see page 9)
¹/₂ cup raw organic agave nectar
2 vanilla beans, split and scraped (see page 15)
3 organic apricot kernels (see page 8)
¹/₄ to ¹/₂ teaspoon spirulina powder for color (optional, see page 15)

MAKES ABOUT 1 QUART

Combine the pistachio milk, coconut milk, agave nectar, scraped vanilla bean seeds, apricot kernels, and spirulina in a blender. Blend on high until silky smooth, at least 1 minute.

Place the blender in the freezer for 40 minutes to 1 hour or in the refrigerator for at least 1 hour or up to overnight, until well chilled. Pour the mixture into an ice cream maker and freeze according to the manufacturer's instructions. Serve immediately or transfer to airtight containers and store in the freezer until ready to serve.

Also known as the filbert, the hazelnut has a wonderfully unique nutty flavor that is often used in cakes, liqueur, and coffee. In the United States, hazelnuts are grown in the Northwest, including here in my home state of Washington. In this recipe, I combine hazelnut milk with another one of our locally grown stars, the amazing cherry.

Hazelnut Cherry

2 cups hazelnut milk (page 14)
2 cups packed organic pitted Bing, Lambert, or Rainier cherries
1/2 cup packed organic pitted Medjool dates (see page 7)

MAKES ABOUT 1 QUART

Combine the hazelnut milk and 1 cup of the cherries in a blender. Blend until smooth. With the motor running, gradually add the dates and blend on high until silky smooth, at least 1 minute. Place the blender in the freezer for 40 minutes to 1 hour or in the refrigerator for at least 1 hour or up to overnight, until well chilled.

Chop the remaining 1 cup cherries and place in the freezer to chill.

Pour the hazelnut-cherry mixture into an ice cream maker and freeze according to the manufacturer's instructions. Remove the cover and blade from the ice cream maker and fold in the chopped cherries, distributing evenly. Serve immediately or transfer to airtight containers and store in the freezer until ready to serve.

Whenever I need a quick, healthy, and tasty snack on the go,
I reach for a handful of almonds and a ripe banana. The almonds
offer a satisfying nutty flavor, while the banana brings a tropical
sweetness to the mix. It was natural for me to create an ice cream
with this pleasing combination. Garnish with chopped almonds.

Banana Almond

2 cups almond milk (page 13)
2 cups mashed overripe organic bananas (about 4 bananas)

MAKES ABOUT 1 QUART

Combine the almond milk and bananas in a blender. Blend on
high until silky smooth, at least 1 minute.

Place the blender in the freezer for 40 minutes to 1 hour
or in the refrigerator for at least 1 hour or up to overnight,
until well chilled. Pour the mixture into an ice cream maker
and freeze according to the manufacturer's instructions. Serve
immediately or transfer to airtight containers and store in the
freezer until ready to serve.

While traditional vanilla may be the all-time most popular ice cream flavor, adding coconut water to the mix enhances the taste and works magic with the fresh vanilla. Drizzle Chocolate Sauce (page 120) on top and garnish with chopped nuts.

Raw Vanilla

2 vanilla beans, sliced and scraped (see page 15)
2^1/$_2$ cups young coconut water (see page 11)
1 cup raw organic cashews or cashew pieces
^{3}/$_4$ cup packed organic pitted honey dates (see page 7)

MAKES ABOUT 1 QUART

Combine the scraped vanilla bean seeds, coconut water, and cashews in a blender. Blend until smooth. With the motor running, gradually add the dates and blend on high until silky smooth, at least 1 minute.

Place the blender in the freezer for 40 minutes to 1 hour or in the refrigerator for at least 1 hour or up to overnight, until well chilled. Pour the mixture into an ice cream maker and freeze according to the manufacturer's instructions. Serve immediately or transfer to airtight containers and store in the freezer until ready to serve.

This is another lovely variation of vanilla. The hazelnut offers a unique rich sweetness. Those sensitive to other nuts may find hazelnut milk to be their preferred ice cream base. Garnish with your choice of sauce (see pages 118–28) or fresh fruit, along with chopped hazelnuts.

Vanilla Hazelnut

2 vanilla beans, sliced and scraped (see page 15)
2^1/$_2$ cups hazelnut milk (page 14)
1^1/$_2$ cups packed organic pitted honey dates (see page 7)

MAKES ABOUT 1 QUART

Combine the scraped vanilla bean seeds and hazelnut milk in a blender. With the motor running, gradually add the dates and blend on high until silky smooth, at least 1 minute.

Place the blender in the freezer for 40 minutes to 1 hour or in the refrigerator for at least 1 hour or up to overnight, until well chilled. Pour the mixture into an ice cream maker and freeze according to the manufacturer's instructions. Serve immediately or transfer to airtight containers and store in the freezer until ready to serve.

Creamy, soothing, and delicious . . . fresh coconut milk
is an amazing flavor to me. Add some dates and fresh
vanilla, and you have an exquisite ice cream. Eat this
on its own or with your favorite topping.

Coconut Vanilla

3 vanilla beans, sliced and scraped (see page 15)
3 cups fresh coconut milk (see page 9)
1 cup packed organic pitted Medjool dates (see page 7)

MAKES ABOUT 1 QUART

Combine the scraped vanilla bean seeds and coconut milk
in a blender. With the motor running, gradually add the dates
and blend on high until silky smooth, at least 1 minute.

Place the blender in the freezer for 40 minutes to 1 hour
or in the refrigerator for at least 1 hour or up to overnight,
until well chilled. Pour the mixture into an ice cream maker
and freeze according to the manufacturer's instructions. Serve
immediately or transfer to airtight containers and store in the
freezer until ready to serve.

The almond has been revered for thousands of years. Sweetening fresh almond milk with dates—an ancient fruit in its own right—is a natural pairing. Try this ice cream over a vegan brownie and top with Chocolate Sauce (page 120) and garnish with chopped almonds.

Almond Date

3 cups almond milk (page 13)
1 cup packed organic pitted honey dates (see page 7)

MAKES ABOUT 1 QUART

Put the almond milk in a blender. With the motor running, gradually add the dates and blend on high until silky smooth, at least 1 minute.

Place the blender in the freezer for 40 minutes to 1 hour or in the refrigerator for at least 1 hour or up to overnight, until well chilled. Pour the mixture into an ice cream maker and freeze according to the manufacturer's instructions. Serve immediately or transfer to airtight containers and store in the freezer until ready to serve.

As amazing as chocolate may be to many of us, some may prefer subtler flavors, while others may be sensitive to the theobromine found in chocolate. Sweet, earthy carob is a wonderful alternative. It is flavorful and doesn't have stimulating effects like chocolate does. Garnish with chopped nuts.

Raw Carob

2¹/₂ cups coconut water (see page 11)
1 cup raw organic cashews or cashew pieces
³/₄ cup packed organic pitted honey dates (see page 7)
¹/₂ cup unsweetened carob powder

MAKES ABOUT 1 QUART

Combine the coconut water and cashews in a blender. Blend until smooth. With the motor running, gradually add the dates and blend on high until silky smooth, at least 1 minute. With the motor running, add the carob powder and blend until evenly distributed.

Place the blender in the freezer for 40 minutes to 1 hour or in the refrigerator for at least 1 hour or up to overnight, until well chilled. Pour the mixture into an ice cream maker and freeze according to the manufacturer's instructions. Serve immediately or transfer to airtight containers and store in the freezer until ready to serve.

RAW CACAO Replace the carob powder with raw organic cacao powder.

In this effortlessly delicious recipe, rich, creamy fresh coconut milk is balanced by its perfect foil—robust, chocolaty carob. Garnish with shredded coconut.

Coconut Carob

3 cups fresh coconut milk (see page 9)
1 cup packed organic pitted black dates (see page 7)
$^1/_2$ cup unsweetened carob powder

MAKES ABOUT 1 QUART

Put the coconut milk in a blender. With the motor running, gradually add the dates and blend on high until silky smooth, at least 1 minute. With the motor running, add the carob powder and blend until evenly distributed.

Place the blender in the freezer for 40 minutes to 1 hour or in the refrigerator for at least 1 hour or up to overnight, until well chilled. Pour the mixture into an ice cream maker and freeze according to the manufacturer's instructions. Serve immediately or transfer to airtight containers and store in the freezer until ready to serve.

ALMOND CAROB Replace the coconut milk with 3 cups almond milk (page 13).

COCONUT CACAO Replace the carob powder with raw organic cacao powder.

Like the German torte of the same name, this ice cream
layers crisp fresh cherries and luxurious, rich chocolate for
a decadent treat. Garnish with sliced fresh cherries.

Raw Black Forest

$^3/_4$ cup packed organic pitted black dates (see page 7)
$^3/_4$ cup purified water or coconut water (see page 11)
1$^3/_4$ pounds organic Bing, Lambert, or Rainier cherries, pitted,
plus 1 cup chopped pitted cherries
1 cup raw organic cashews or cashew pieces
$^1/_2$ cup raw organic cacao powder

MAKES ABOUT 1 QUART

Place the dates in a jar, add the water, cover, and refrigerate
overnight. Drain, reserving the sweet soaking liquid.

Run the 1$^3/_4$ pounds cherries through a juicer to make
2 cups juice. Place the chopped cherries in the freezer to chill.

Combine the soaking liquid from the dates, cherry juice,
and cashews in a blender. Blend until smooth. With the motor
running, gradually add the dates and blend on high until silky
smooth, at least 1 minute. With the motor running, add the
cacao powder and blend until evenly distributed. Place the
blender in the freezer for 40 minutes to 1 hour or in the refrigerator for at least 1 hour or up to overnight, until well chilled.

Pour the cherry juice mixture into an ice cream maker and
freeze according to the manufacturer's instructions. Remove
the cover and blade from the ice cream maker and fold in the
chopped cherries, distributing evenly. Serve immediately or
transfer to airtight containers and store in the freezer until
ready to serve.

For many years I have occasionally indulged in a raw vegan Mayan chocolate truffle available at a local health food store. Here I capture its signature flavors of chocolate, cinnamon, and fiery cayenne pepper. Garnish this ice cream with a cinnamon stick.

Mayan Chocolate

3 cups coconut milk (see page 9)
$^1/_2$ cup raw organic cacao powder
1 teaspoon organic cinnamon
1 teaspoon organic cayenne pepper
2 vanilla beans, split and scraped (see page 15)
3 organic apricot kernels (see page 8)
1 tablespoon raw organic coconut oil
$^3/_4$ cup packed organic pitted honey dates (see page 7)

MAKES ABOUT 1 QUART

Combine the coconut milk, cacao powder, cinnamon, cayenne, scraped vanilla bean seeds, apricot kernels, and coconut oil in a blender. Blend until smooth. With the motor running, gradually add the dates and blend on high until silky smooth, at least 1 minute.

Place the blender in the freezer for 40 minutes to 1 hour or in the refrigerator for at least 1 hour or up to overnight, until well chilled. Pour the mixture into an ice cream maker and freeze according to the manufacturer's instructions. Serve immediately or transfer to airtight containers and store in the freezer until ready to serve.

When I was growing up, I always looked forward to eating pecan pie come fall. This recipe brings some of the delicious richness of pecan pie to ice cream. The flavor of pecans is buttery and autumnal, and these warm notes find a cool counterbalance in this refreshing, cold treat.

Pecan Pie

1 cup chopped organic pecans
1 vanilla bean, split and scraped (see page 15)
3 cups pecan milk (page 14)
1 cup packed organic pitted honey dates (see page 7)

MAKES ABOUT 1 QUART

Place the chopped pecans in the freezer to chill.

Combine the scraped vanilla bean seeds and pecan milk in a blender. With the motor running, gradually add the dates and blend on high until silky smooth, at least 1 minute.

Place the blender in the freezer for 40 minutes to 1 hour or in the refrigerator for at least 1 hour or up to overnight, until well chilled. Pour the mixture into an ice cream maker and freeze according to the manufacturer's instructions. Remove the cover and blade from the ice cream maker and fold in the chopped pecans, distributing evenly. Serve immediately or transfer to airtight containers and store in the freezer until ready to serve.

I first made this ice cream over the holidays many years ago. I grew up drinking eggnog during the winter season, but when I gave up eggs in the 1990s, I wasn't able to enjoy the traditional holiday beverage for some time. I decided to make an ice cream to capture the flavor that I missed, combining spices and sweeteners that mimicked the essence and texture of the original. Overripe banana does the trick to round out the flavor and add the creaminess typical of eggnog.

Veggnog

1 vanilla bean, sliced and scraped (see page 15)
3 cups fresh coconut milk (see page 9)
$^{1}/_{4}$ teaspoon ground nutmeg
$^{2}/_{3}$ cup packed organic pitted honey dates (see page 7)
$^{2}/_{3}$ cup mashed slightly overripe organic banana

MAKES ABOUT 1 QUART

Combine the scraped vanilla bean seeds, coconut milk, and nutmeg in a blender. With the motor running, gradually add the dates and blend on high until silky smooth, at least 1 minute. Add the banana and continue blending until creamy.

Place the blender in the freezer for 40 minutes to 1 hour or in the refrigerator for at least 1 hour or up to overnight, until well chilled. Pour the mixture into an ice cream maker and freeze according to the manufacturer's instructions. Serve immediately or transfer to airtight containers and store in the freezer until ready to serve.

In a traditional gingersnap cookie, peppery ginger plays against the rich, syrupy flavor of molasses. In this raw version, we achieve that robust sweetness with black dates. The fresh ginger juice brings some zing to this trio of ingredients!

Raw Gingersnap

3 cups almond milk (page 13)
2 tablespoons fresh organic ginger juice (see page 13)
1 cup packed organic pitted black dates (see page 7)

MAKES ABOUT 1 QUART

Combine the almond milk and ginger juice in a blender. With the motor running, gradually add the dates and blend on high until silky smooth, at least 1 minute.

Place the blender in the freezer for 40 minutes to 1 hour or in the refrigerator for at least 1 hour or up to overnight, until well chilled. Pour the mixture into an ice cream maker and freeze according to the manufacturer's instructions. Serve immediately or transfer to airtight containers and store in the freezer until ready to serve.

In this recipe, I capture the essence of chai by adding the spices that are traditionally used to make the aromatic spicy tea. The coconut water brings it to life, and the cashews give it a lovely creamy flavor and texture. As an alternative, consider using coconut milk in place of the coconut water and cashews. You could also try making a sun tea using a traditional black tea in place of the coconut water.

Chai

2^1/$_2$ cups coconut water (see page 11)
1 cup raw organic cashews or cashew pieces
2 teaspoons minced organic ginger
^{1}/$_2$ teaspoon ground cardamom
^{1}/$_4$ teaspoon ground cloves
^{1}/$_4$ teaspoon ground cinnamon
^{1}/$_4$ teaspoon ground allspice
^{3}/$_4$ cup packed organic pitted honey dates (see page 7)

MAKES ABOUT 1 QUART

Combine the coconut water, cashews, ginger, cardamom, cloves, cinnamon, and allspice in a blender. Blend on high until silky smooth, at least 1 minute. With the motor running, gradually add the dates and continue blending until smooth.

Place the blender in the freezer for 40 minutes to 1 hour or in the refrigerator for at least 1 hour or up to overnight, until well chilled. Pour the mixture into an ice cream maker and freeze according to the manufacturer's instructions. Serve immediately or transfer to airtight containers and store in the freezer until ready to serve.

This is a fun and fresh spicy ice cream. Use just the right amount of heat for you. Just 1 teaspoon of jalapeño will give the ice cream a slight flavor with a little kick. Adding a second teaspoon will give you more heat, and 3 teaspoons will deliver quite a punch. The coldness of the ice cream and the fiery heat of the jalapeño create a delightful combination.

Raw Jalapeño Heaven

1 to 3 teaspoons minced organic jalapeño
3 cups purified water
1 cup raw organic cashews or cashew pieces
1 cup packed organic pitted Medjool dates (see page 7)

MAKES ABOUT 1 QUART

Combine the jalapeño, water, and cashews in a blender. Blend on high until silky smooth, at least 1 minute. With the motor running, gradually add the dates and continue blending until smooth.

Place the blender in the freezer for 40 minutes to 1 hour or in the refrigerator for at least 1 hour or up to overnight, until well chilled. Pour the mixture into an ice cream maker and freeze according to the manufacturer's instructions. Serve immediately or transfer to airtight containers and store in the freezer until ready to serve.

SAUCES

A dark, chocolaty sauce is the most fundamental recipe in an ice cream topping repertoire. Chocolate and carob sauces (pictured on page 123) are delicious served over many of the ice creams in this book. Experiment by pairing them with classic and unexpected ice cream flavors, whether over a single scoop or a banana split!

Carob or Chocolate Sauce

½ cup organic cashews or cashew pieces
1½ cups coconut water (see page 11), plus more as needed
½ cup packed organic pitted honey dates (see page 7)
¾ cup carob powder or raw organic cacao powder

MAKES ABOUT 2½ CUPS

Combine the cashews and coconut water in a blender. Blend on high until silky smooth, at least 1 minute. With the motor running, gradually add the dates and blend until smooth. (Dates vary in water content, so you may need to add more coconut water to achieve a smooth consistency.) Add the carob or cacao powder and blend until evenly distributed. Serve over the ice cream of your choice. Store refrigerated, in an airtight container, for up to 3 days.

While this sauce has the creamy, tropical flavor of coconut you'd expect, it also has definite caramel notes. Try this sauce by itself over ice cream or in combination with other sauces. This sauce will work with lighter flavored ice cream, such as Strawberry (page 45) and can work especially well with a robust ice cream, such as Chocolate (page 25).

Coconut Sauce

$2/3$ cup fresh coconut milk (see page 9)
$1/3$ cup packed organic pitted honey dates (see page 7)

MAKES 1 CUP

Put the coconut milk in a blender. A 1-cup blender jar works best (see page 19). With the motor running, gradually add the dates and blend on high until silky smooth, at least 1 minute. Serve over the ice cream of your choice. Store refrigerated, in an airtight container, for up to 3 days.

Colorful and fruity, strawberry sauce is a wonderful topping on ice creams and is a classic over vanilla. It is also a must-have over banana splits. Strawberries can vary in their flavor, sweetness, and water content, so balance the dates and berries to taste and texture.

Strawberry Sauce

1¹/₂ cups packed hulled organic strawberries
¹/₃ cup packed organic pitted honey dates (see page 7)

MAKES 1 CUP

Run the strawberries through a juicer to make ²/₃ cup juice. Alternatively, you can puree the strawberries in a blender.

Put the strawberry juice in a blender. A 1-cup blender jar works best (see page 19). With the motor running, gradually add the dates and blend on high until silky smooth, at least 1 minute. Serve over the ice cream of your choice. Store refrigerated, in an airtight container, for up to 3 days.

Left to right:
Strawberry Sauce, Carob
Sauce (page 120), and
Mango Sauce (page 127)

This strawberry sauce variation makes use of the mild, pleasant flavor profile of coconut water. Try it with ice creams such as Almond (page 40), as well as the exotic Coconut Durian (page 86).

Strawberry Sauce Too

¹/₂ cup packed hulled organic strawberries
¹/₄ cup coconut water (see page 11), plus more as needed
¹/₄ cup packed organic pitted honey dates (see page 7)

MAKES 1 CUP

Combine the strawberries and coconut water in a blender. A 1-cup blender jar works best (see page 19). With the motor running, gradually add the dates and blend on high until silky smooth, at least 1 minute. (Dates vary in water content, so you may need to add more coconut water to achieve a smooth consistency.) Serve over the ice cream of your choice. Store refrigerated, in an airtight container, for up to 3 days.

Reminiscent of the jam my mother made fresh from just-picked raspberries from our backyard, this sauce offers a luscious berry flavor to your desserts. The classic combination is with vanilla ice cream, but get creative and experiment by pairing it with any number of other flavors!

Raspberry Sauce

$1/4$ cup packed organic raspberries
$1/2$ cup coconut water (see page 11) or purified water, plus more as needed
$1/4$ cup packed organic pitted honey dates (see page 7)

MAKES 1 CUP

Combine the raspberries and coconut water in a blender. A 1-cup blender jar works best (see page 19). With the motor running, gradually add the dates and blend on high until silky smooth, at least 1 minute. (Dates vary in water content, so you may need to add more coconut water to achieve a smooth consistency.) Serve over the ice cream of your choice. Store refrigerated, in an airtight container, for up to 3 days.

This sauce offers a lovely tropical flavor and a jolt of golden color to your ice creams. Consider partnering this sauce with the Coconut Sauce (page 121).

Mango Sauce

1¹/₂ cups sliced peeled organic mango
¹/₃ cup packed organic pitted honey dates (see page 7)

MAKES 1 CUP

Run the mango through a juicer to make ²⁄₃ cup juice. Alternatively, you can blend the mango without juicing.

Put the mango juice in a blender. A 1-cup blender jar works best (see page 19). With the motor running, gradually add the dates and blend on high until silky smooth, at least 1 minute. Serve over the ice cream of your choice. Store refrigerated, in an airtight container, for up to 3 days.

Back to front:
Strawberry Sauce (page 122),
Carob Sauce (page 120),
Blueberry Sauce (page 128),
and Mango Sauce

This striking deep purple sauce (pictured on page 126) brings an unexpected color to your ice cream dishes. Try it layered with Blueberry ice cream (page 48) in ice pop molds. As with other fruits, the flavor, sweetness, and water content of blueberries may vary, so balance the ingredients as necessary and add a little purified water if needed.

Blueberry Sauce

1½ cups organic blueberries
⅓ cup packed organic pitted honey dates (see page 7)

MAKES 1 CUP

Run the blueberries through a juicer to make ⅔ cup juice. Alternatively, you can blend the blueberries without juicing.

Put the blueberry juice in a blender. A 1-cup blender jar works best (see page 19). With the motor running, gradually add the dates and blend on high until silky smooth, at least 1 minute. Serve over the ice cream of your choice. Store refrigerated, in an airtight container, for up to 3 days.

About the Author

JEFF ROGERS grew up in Stowe, Vermont, where he became interested in food and tourism. After working at a popular restaurant, he moved to New Hampshire to study hotel and restaurant management at college. While pursuing a career in hotels, he honed his skills in the kitchen by experimenting and creating recipes of his own.

Adapting his diet to improve his health, he eventually became a vegan, eschewing all animal products. But he still craved the premium dairy ice creams he once ate and so used his kitchen gifts to experiment with creating a rich, gourmet vegan ice cream. As he became interested in the raw food movement, he also began to make ice creams with all raw ingredients.

Soon after beginning his vegan ice cream venture, Jeff began sharing his desserts with friends. A physician friend noted that in a world where people are trying to eat low-fat foods and fewer sweets, it was naughty of Jeff to create these decadent desserts, vegan or not. Thus, he was dubbed "The Naughty Vegan" and has used the nickname ever since.

Jeff has volunteered for and done pro bono work for animal rights, vegan, and raw food groups, including People for the Ethical Treatment of Animal (PETA), Northwest Animal Rights Network (NARN), Farm Sanctuary, the Gentle Barn, Raw Network of Washington, and EarthSave.

Jeff has been a speaker at International Raw & Living Foods Festivals (Portland, Oregon), Raw & Living Spirit Retreats (Molalla, Oregon), Taste of Health Festivals (Vancouver, British Columbia, and New York City), Portland VegFest (Oregon), Vegetarian Summerfest (Pennsylvania), and the Toronto Vegetarian Food Festival.

Jeff has exhibited at WorldFest (Los Angeles) many times, as well as at Animal Rights National Conference 2007 (Los Angeles). He also had a booth at the 2001 PETA Gala in New York City and was a volunteer for Chef Tal Ronnen and others at the 2005 PETA 25th Anniversary Gala in Los Angeles.

PETA awarded Jeff a Proggy Award for the "Best Dessert Cookbook" for *Vice Cream* in 2004.

You can learn more about Jeff and his ice cream by visiting his website, TheNaughtyVegan.com. You'll also find information on equipment (like how to choose an ice cream maker) and gadgets on this site.

Jeff actively promotes the awareness of the benefits of a plant-based diet so that people may make informed choices regarding their diet and health. Jeff has started a variety of projects, such as the SoyStache and Drumming Instead projects, as well as Jeff's Buttons, and has created and maintains many websites. Jeff has been an avid photographer since high school and writes poetry. See his photography and learn more about his other projects at JeffRogers.us.

Measurement Conversion Charts

VOLUME

U.S.	IMPERIAL	METRIC
1 tablespoon	$^1/_2$ fl oz	15 ml
2 tablespoons	1 fl oz	30 ml
$^1/_4$ cup	2 fl oz	60 ml
$^1/_3$ cup	3 fl oz	90 ml
$^1/_2$ cup	4 fl oz	120 ml
$^2/_3$ cup	5 fl oz ($^1/_4$ pint)	150 ml
$^3/_4$ cup	6 fl oz	180 ml
1 cup	8 fl oz ($^1/_3$ pint)	240 ml
$1^1/_4$ cups	10 fl oz ($^1/_2$ pint)	300 ml
2 cups (1 pint)	16 fl oz ($^2/_3$ pint)	480 ml
$2^1/_2$ cups	20 fl oz (1 pint)	600 ml
1 quart	32 fl oz ($1^2/_3$ pints)	1 l

TEMPERATURE

FAHRENHEIT	CELSIUS/ GAS MARK
250°F	120°C/gas mark $^1/_2$
275°F	135°C/gas mark 1
300°F	150°C/gas mark 2
325°F	160°C/gas mark 3
350°F	180 or 175°C/ gas mark 4
375°F	190°C/gas mark 5
400°F	200°C/gas mark 6
425°F	220°C/gas mark 7
450°F	230°C/gas mark 8
475°F	245°C/gas mark 9
500°F	260°C

LENGTH

INCH	METRIC
$^1/_4$ inch	6 mm
$^1/_2$ inch	1.25 cm
$^3/_4$ inch	2 cm
1 inch	2.5 cm
6 inches ($^1/_2$ foot)	15 cm
12 inches (1 foot)	30 cm

WEIGHT

U.S./IMPERIAL	METRIC
$^1/_2$ oz	15 g
1 oz	30 g
2 oz	60 g
$^1/_4$ lb	115 g
$^1/_3$ lb	150 g
$^1/_2$ lb	225 g
$^3/_4$ lb	350 g
1 lb	450 g

Index

Originally published in the United States in somewhat different form
as *Vice Cream*, by Celestial Arts, Berkeley, in 2004.

Library of Congress Cataloging-in-Publication Data
Rogers, Jeff, 1961-
  [Vice cream]
  Vegan ice cream : over 90 sinfully delicious dairy-free delights /
Jeff Rogers.
    pages cm
  Revised edition of Vice Cream.
  1. Ice cream, ices, etc. 2. Vegan cooking. I. Title.
  TX795.R586 2014
  641.86'2—dc23
                                    2013040160
Hardcover ISBN: 978-1-60774-545-7
eBook ISBN: 978-1-60774-546-4

Printed in China

Design by Chloe Rawlins
Food styling by Julie Hopper

10 9 8 7 6 5 4 3 2 1

Revised Edition